All You Need to Know About Bidding

Also by Terence Reese and David Bird

Bridge – Tricks of the Trade

Miracles of Card Play

Unholy Tricks
More Miraculous Card Play

Doubled and Venerable
Further Miracles of Card Play

Cardinal Sins

All You Need to Know About Bidding

Terence Reese and David Bird

London
VICTOR GOLLANCZ LTD
in association with
PETER CRAWLEY

First published in Great Britain 1992
in association with Peter Crawley
by Victor Gollancz Ltd
14 Henrietta Street, London WC2E 8QJ

ISBN 0 575 05378 X

Photoset in Great Britain by
Rowland Phototypesetting Ltd,
Bury St Edmunds, Suffolk
and printed by St Edmundsbury Press Ltd,
Bury St Edmunds, Suffolk

Contents

Foreword

There was a time when a fairly complete account of bidding technique could be presented in the 120 or so pages that are the length of this book. No longer. The game has become more complex and styles differ in all parts of the world.

In this book we have concentrated on *standard* methods for *standard* players, those who are neither beginners nor over-inventive experts. Our target has been the average player who is accustomed to finishing about half way in local tournaments. All he (or she) will need to enter the upper ranges is to acquire a good understanding of modern bidding styles.

By way of a novelty, Chapter 13, which deals with the relative worth of part score and game, game and slam, defending and competing, may surprise you.

Terence Reese
David Bird

Should I Open on This?

You might think it was easy to tell whether a particular hand was worth an opening bid. In fact players of several years' experience still tend to make poor decisions in this area.

How would you rate this borderline specimen, for example?

(1)   ♠ KQ10854   ♡ 7   ♢ 964   ♣ AJ3

Players of the type who 'don't like to open on less than 12 points, partner' would give this hand a miss. Of course, you should open at any score. You have six good cards in spades, the senior suit, and by speaking first you make life harder for the opponents.

(2)   ♠ J9763   ♡ 875   ♢ KQ   ♣ AQ2

Here you have 12 points but most of them are in the short suits, always a bad sign. Nor will you necessarily want partner to lead a spade if the opponents end up playing the hand. It's best to pass on such hands.

Even if your style is to play a weak notrump (12–14) it is best to pass in the first two positions when you hold an unimpressive 12-pointer such as:

(3)   ♠ K85   ♡ J64   ♢ KJ72   ♣ A63

You will scarcely ever miss game by passing this type of hand and this is certainly the best tactics at teams or rubber bridge. In pairs it is common to open such hands, hoping for a small plus score when the outstanding points are evenly spread. What benefit this brings is doubtful.

Suppose you hold the same hand in third position. Game is unlikely, so you should be wary of exposing yourself to a double by opening a weak notrump. Since you don't now have to prepare a rebid it is reasonable, at pairs, to open 1◇; you will pass any response by partner.

When you have some shape in third position, it is always tempting to open light. The weaker you are, the more the fourth player is likely to hold. In a borderline case always consider the strength of the suit which you intend to open. You are likely to be outgunned in the auction after all, and partner will then tend lead the suit you have named.

Suppose, after two passes, you hold this hand:

(4)   ♠ Q6   ♡ KJ852   ◇ A863   ♣ 75

Open 1♡. At tournament play you could even risk the call when vulnerable. You will pass any response from partner and, if the opponents win the auction, your opening may attract a good lead. The reason for opening is not so much that you expect to make a plus score as that accurate bidding, in general, is more difficult when an opponent has opened.

(5)   ♠ KQJ72   ♡ 4   ◇ 752   ♣ K1073

Only 9 points but again you should open in the third position, here with 1♠. If partner is in an inconvenient mood and responds 2♡, you must pass. If you rebid 2♠ partner may inconveniently follow with 2NT or even 3NT and the axe may fall.

The situation is different on a collection like this:

(6)   ♠ K83   ♡ 5   ◇ Q10642   ♣ AJ54

You are strong enough for a third-seat opening and many players would go ahead and open 1◇. Such calls are losing bridge, though. You're hardly likely to take the bread out of anyone's mouth with a low call like 1◇. Nor, if your left-hand opponent plays the contract eventually, do you want to insist on a diamond lead. Finally, partner 'always' responds 1♡. It is best to pass.

The pre-emptive value of one in a minor is so negligible that in the third seat it is sometimes tempting to risk a three bid when well short of the normal requirements.

(7)　　　♠ 32　　　♡ 84　　　♢ QJ92　　　♣ KQJ92

This is the sort of hand where you would not be surprised to end up defending against a major-suit game. When non-vulnerable you can afford to make life difficult for your left-hand opponent by opening 3♣.

In the fourth seat, after three passes, the question to ask yourself when confronted with a borderline opening is 'Are we likely to win the auction?' If the answer is no, which is most likely to be the case when you are short in spades, it may be best to pass even when you hold the values for a bid.

(8)　　　♠ 3　　　♡ AJ76　　　♢ J32　　　♣ AQ964

You have 12 points and a good suit and would certainly open 1♣ in any of the first three seats. In fourth, though, you must think twice. The opponents are likely to hold around half the points in the pack, together with a fair spade fit. If you start the auction rolling with 1♣, it will be no surprise to hear a 1♠ overcall on your left. The prudent course is to pass.

For those who like to reduce bridge to a set of 'rules' (not our general idea of how to bid, we may say) you can add your points to the number of spades you have. If the total comes to 15 or more, you can open the bidding in fourth seat. Here you have 12 points and 1 spade, leaving you short of the requirements.

When you are short in spades but have a good suit elsewhere, it may be possible to grab the part score by opening with an over-strength three bid.

(9)　　　♠ 7　　　♡ K54　　　♢ AQ10932　　　♣ Q96

Here indisputably you have the values to open. In fourth position, though, you would be worried that a 1♢ opening might let the enemy get together in spades. It's good tactics to raise the ante by opening such hands 3♢. The same bid can work well in third position, too. You *might* miss a good 3NT contract when partner had a maximum pass; much more likely is that the fourth player will have a good hand and be inconvenienced by your call.

In fourth position it is less dangerous to open a 12-point balanced hand, or an 11-point hand with fair spades, than it would be in the first two seats. This is assuming, of course, that you are not playing with one of those idiots who jump to 3NT 'because I had passed originally'.

(10)   ♠ KQ1093   ♡ K86   ◇ K62   ♣ 43

You would hesitate to open this in the first two seats because you would have to find a rebid and partner might then carry you too high. In fourth position, facing a passed partner, there is no need to find a rebid. It is reasonable to open 1♠.

You may have observed that tournament players sometimes open on rather poor hands, worse even than some of the dubious specimens we have inspected above. This is partly because in tournament play, especially pairs play, small gains are important; and partly because they think that their devilishly good judgement will enable them to do the right thing in close situations. To set against that is a point that is consistently overlooked: the less wide the range of your opening bids, the more accurate all your constructive bidding is likely to be. You don't want your partner to think all the time, 'I had better hold back a bit in case he's opened on his usual rubbish'.

Problems in Response

In this chapter we will concentrate on three areas where errors are frequent:

1. the response on poor hands;
2. the response on two-suiters;
3. when to make a jump shift.

The response on poor hands

Since an opening bid at the one level may contain 19 points, and 25 points is regarded as the benchmark for game, the standard for responding to a one-bid has been set at 6 points or more. In truth there are many occasions when it is better to pass on a 6-count.

Suppose partner has opened 1♠ and you hold:

(1)   ♠ 53   ♡ 6   ◇ Q8742   ♣ KJ653

You can hardly bid at the two level with 6 points; the standard for a two-level response nowadays is nearer to 10 points, or a good 9. A 1NT response is decidedly unattractive with a singleton heart; partner will doubtless rebid 2♡, or even 3♡. Even if you strike lucky and he passes your 1NT response, there is little reason to think that 1NT will play any better than 1♠.

The only sensible course is to pass. If the opponents now enter the bidding and their auction dies out in 2♡, you will have the chance to compete with a take-out double, suggesting values in the unbid suits and some tolerance for spades.

(2)   ♠ 7   ♡ Q32   ◇ KJ10842   ♣ 965

On this type of hand, too, it is advisable to pass. You may have the opportunity to show the long suit later.

When you do choose to respond 1NT to 1♡ or 1♠, the normal standard is 6–9 points; when partner has opened 1♣ or 1♢, a 1NT response shows more like 7–10. Suppose partner opens 1♢; how do you view responding hands such as these:

or

| (3) | ♠ Q43 | ♡ 10652 | ♢ J94 | ♣ A83 |

| (4) | ♠ J762 | ♡ Q54 | ♢ 94 | ♣ KJ85 |

Many players would respond 1♡ on (3) and 1♠ on (4). 'You must show a four-card major,' they will chant. This is a poor idea when the major is so weak; if partner raises you on 3-card support the contract will play awkwardly. On hands of this type it is far more sensible to respond 1NT. Take away a jack, leaving you with a barren 6-count, and you would be too weak for 1NT over 1♢; on hands of that type it is best to pass.

It's not so bad to make a noise of some kind when you hold support for partner's suit. Partner opens 1♠ and you hold:

or

| (5) | ♠ J843 | ♡ K4 | ♢ 752 | ♣ 8643 |

| (6) | ♠ 9742 | ♡ 5 | ♢ Q8752 | ♣ 1063 |

Most players would raise to 2♠ on either of these. You will probably lose points in the end, but it will be in a good cause. The opponents are marked with fair values and will have a promising fit somewhere themselves.

The response on two-suiters

There is no problem in response when you hold two 4-card suits; you bid the lower one first. Suppose partner opens 1♣ and you hold:

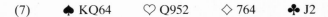

| (7) | ♠ KQ64 | ♡ Q952 | ♢ 764 | ♣ J2 |

You respond 1♡, despite that suit being weaker than the spades. This clearly gives your side the best chance to discover a 4–4 fit.

The problem comes when you have a 5-card minor and a 4-card major. Which suit should you call? Suppose partner has opened 1♢ and you hold:

(8)   ♠ K1063   ♡ Q5   ♢ 84   ♣ K7632

Here you are below strength for a two-level response, which nowadays promises nearer 10 points than 8. You have to respond 1♠ and the clubs will probably never see the light of day.

Now make the hand a bit stronger:

(9)   ♠ KJ72   ♡ 95   ♢ 87   ♣ AQ943

You have the values to bid at the two-level, so is 2♣ right? It's doubtful, because after 1♡ – 2♣ – 2♡ you are not strong enough to make a second call; you would have to pass. In this situation it is again right to respond 1♠.

Add another point or two and the hand is strong enough to make two calls:

(10)   ♠ KQ76   ♡ 7   ♢ 1062   ♣ AQ1072

Now you should respond 2♣, intending to continue with 2♠ if partner rebids 2♡. One of the minor mysteries of the game is why American players, in particular, invariably respond in the major on these occasions. When you have the strength to make two calls it is obviously best to bid your suits in the natural way, showing partner your suit lengths. On the present hand 1♡ – 1♠ – 2♡ would be a most undesirable sequence, since a continuation of 3♣ would both exaggerate your strength and suggest five cards in the spade suit.

When responder holds a 5–5 hand the general rule is to bid the higher suit first. Partner opens 1♣ and you hold:

(11)   ♠ J7653   ♡ 5   ♢ AKQ104   ♣ J3

It is a mistake to respond 1♢ because the suit is stronger. If you don't introduce the spades at once it may be difficult to tell partner that you hold five. It is more important to locate major-suit fits than those in a minor.

Also, and perhaps this will surprise you, it is better to settle in the weaker of two suits when the combined length is the same.

Responding hands with 5–6 distribution present a small problem. On moderate hands it will often be wise to name the higher (5-card) suit first. Suppose partner opens 1♣ and you hold this unwieldy specimen:

(12)   ♠ KJ852   ♡ Q107652   ◇ Q   ♣ 4

On most hands a 1♠ response will work out better than 1♡. If he rebids 2♣ you can go to 2♡, offering him a choice of suits. Had partner opened 1◇ instead, then a 1♠ response would not be so attractive; you would not be happy to hear a 2♣ rebid. Over 1◇ respond 1♡, therefore, intending to bale out in 2♡ if partner rebids 2♣ (you would pass a rebid of 2◇).

Make the hand a bit stronger:

(13)   ♠ AQ943   ♡ KJ10852   ◇ K3   ♣ –

Now you are powerful enough to make several bids. You can therefore bid your suits in the natural order. Start with 1♡ and aim to bid spades twice later.

When to make a jump shift

In early books you will find a recommendation to give a jump response on almost all hands of 16 points or more. This tends to be wrong when you are short in partner's suit and need time for development. Many players follow the principle that you should force only on these three hand types:

(a)   hands with excellent trump support;
(b)   strong single-suiters;
(c)   strong balanced hands containing a fair suit.

With other strong hands you should take things more slowly. Suppose partner opens 1♡ and you hold:

(14)   ♠ A74   ♡ 6   ◇ KQ105   ♣ AK843

You need time to express this hand and should start with 2♣. If partner rebids 2♡ you continue with 3◇; you have gone some way towards describing your hand and the bidding is still under control. After a start of 1♡ – 3♣ – 3♡ you would not be so well placed. You would have to shut up shop with 3NT.

The same is true if you have a more marked two-suiter.

(15)   ♠ AK975   ♡ 8   ◇ KQ10854   ♣ A

When partner opens 1♡, you should start with just 2◇. Over a 2♡ rebid you can continue with 2♠. The bidding is still conveniently low and a call of 3♠ on the next round will put you well on the way to describing your hand. When you need several calls to describe your shape you cannot afford to lose space with an initial jump.

Most tournament players make it a firm rule not to force on a two-suiter. What meaning, then, can be assigned to East's second bid in this sequence?

West	East
1♡	3◇
3♡	4♣

Since East cannot hold a minor two-suiter the four-club call will be a cue bid, agreeing hearts as trumps. East might hold this hand:

(16)   ♠ Q   ♡ KJ97   ◇ AQ8742   ♣ A3

If West can now cue-bid 4◇, indicating the king, the playing strength for a slam will surely be there. We will look further at slam bidding in Chapter 9.

Finally let's look at a powerful one-suiter. Partner opens 1♡ and you hold:

(17)   ♠ AQJ9875   ♡ J4   ◇ Q3   ♣ KQ

When this hand was quoted in some magazine competition the question was . . . How should you continue after a start of 1♡ – 1♠ – 2◇? Well, you can jump out of the window. A call of 3♠ would be non-forcing, so you would have to resort to a fourth-suit call of 3♣ (see Chapter 5), not beginning to describe your hand. Surely it is better to respond 2♠ on the first round, showing your strength with one bold brush stroke. You will then follow with 3♠ and 4♠, leaving any further move to partner.

Some American players, and others, force only when they hold something like a solid suit and upwards of four honour tricks. It is silly to put the requirements so high. As Culbertson pointed out sixty years ago, you save neither time nor space by 'keeping it low'; you have to jump on the next round or bid foolishly round the clock, giving no picture of where your values lie.

Support When You Can

A player who has opened with one of a major, especially, will always be pleased if you can support his suit, not necessarily on the first round, but soon after. We deal with this subject under the following headings:

1. Direct raise of a major suit.
2. Direct raise of a minor suit.
3. Manoeuvres after partner has raised.
4. Support on the second round.

Direct raise of a major suit

For a response of 1NT to 1♡ or 1♠ you require, as a rule, about 6 to 9 points. When you are raising a major suit, points don't come into it. These are a few examples of hands where you would raise 1♡ to 2♡:

(1) ♠ J63 ♡ 10742 ◇ 5 ♣ J8643

Vulnerable or not, you need not hesitate to raise to 2♡.

(2) ♠ K4 ♡ Q72 ◇ J843 ♣ 9762

Here 1NT would not be far wrong, but 2♡ is better. Partner will usually hold five hearts for his opening and your hand contains a ruffing value.

(3) ♠ Q852 ♡ J93 ◇ A1064 ♣ 92

Many players, taught to announce a 4-card major, would respond 1♠; but when a hand is worth just one constructive response it is better to raise partner's suit. You may think that you can achieve both goals by following a sequence such as 1♡ – 1♠ – 2♣ – 2♡. As we will see in a moment, though, you often have to follow this sequence when you hold only a doubleton in hearts.

For a double raise of partner's major the standard is about 8 to 11 points, usually including 4-card trump support. Say now that partner has opened 1♠ and you hold:

(4)   ♠ Q1072   ♡ K5   ◇ 1073   ♣ A874

This is dead centre for a raise to three. Add a well-placed queen and you would be on the brink of four spades.

(5)   ♠ J8632   ♡ 4   ◇ A1085   ♣ J32

Not much in high cards but again well worth a raise to three. Non-vulnerable against vulnerable opponents, a partly defensive raise to four would be sound tactics.

(6)   ♠ 10653   ♡ AJ4   ◇ K95   ♣ QJ8

On this hand neither 3♠ nor 2NT could be much criticised.

To raise to game in partner's major suit you would prefer to be about a queen stronger than in the last set of examples. However, there are also hands on which you might raise to game for tactical reasons. Suppose partner opens 1♡, the next player passes, and you hold:

(7)   ♠ 65   ♡ Q10862   ◇ A9743   ♣ 5

Since you have a big fit, it is very likely (indeed, it is a mathematical certainty) that the opponents have one too. You should raise to 4♡, perhaps creating a problem for the opponent on your left. The last thing you should worry about is that this contract may go one down. If it does you can be sure that the opponents had at least a part score their way, probably a game.

2.   Direct raise of a minor suit

We remarked above that when partner has opened one of a major and your hand is worth just one constructive response, preference should be given to a direct raise. This is because the most likely game is four of partner's suit. When partner opens one of a minor the situation is different. Game in notrumps is always a possibility; it may also be necessary to investigate a possible 4–4 fit in a major. So, when partner opens one of a minor you should introduce a major on any *fair* hand, but still raise the minor on a weak hand worth only one call. After partner's 1◇ you hold:

(8)　　　♠ J863　　♡ 107　　◇ K974　　♣ Q82

Here 2◇ is more sensible than 1♠. If partner is blessed with enough strength (upward of 17 points) to proceed towards game, the spade fit will not necessarily be lost.

With fair values, however, usually respond in a major or in notrumps.

(9)　　　♠ A52　　♡ Q1092　　◇ A1073　　♣ J6

Here you respond 1♡ to 1◇. If partner continues with 1♠ or 2♣, you will give jump preference to 3◇; this is invitational but non-forcing.

Suppose you have a different type of hand:

(10)　　　♠ 84　　♡ K9　　◇ A9763　　♣ A842

Here there is no sensible alternative to 3◇.

When you hold exceptional support you may raise to four (or five). This time partner has opened 1♣ and you hold:

(11)　　　♠ 9　　♡ Q753　　◇ J2　　♣ K97542

Go swiftly to 4♣ and hope that the weather keeps fine. Since you are shutting out the possibility of game in notrumps, partner will realise that you are bidding defensively.

3.　Manoeuvres after partner has raised

After a single raise in a major, 1♠ – 2♠, how strong do you think you need to be to try for game? This is one of the most deceptive situations in the game. Suppose that as opener you hold:

(12)   ♠ AQ862   ♡ KJ5   ◇ J3   ♣ A54

Do you think you are worth a try – perhaps 3♠ or 2NT? You are not! You have 15 points, not very powerfully distributed, and partner's average in terms of high cards is not more than about 7 points. You should pass, just as you would after 1♠ – 1NT.

The situation is quite different when you hold strong distribution. Suppose that 1♡ is raised to 2♡ and your hand is:

(13)   ♠ A107   ♡ KQ1085   ◇ 4   ♣ AQ73

You are now worth a 'trial bid' of 3♣. You have no thoughts of playing in clubs, obviously; you are saying to partner: 'Raise to game if you are not minimum'. When partner is uncertain whether he should go to game he will look at his holding in the suit of your trial bid. In particular, if he is short in that suit it will suggest that the two hands fit well; you may be able to take a ruff or two there.

Since it is more helpful to bid three of a new suit when the opener is worth a game try, most players use a call of three of the trump suit as primarily a defensive measure. Suppose you hold this hand and your partner raises 1♡ to 2♡:

(14)   ♠ J   ♡ AQ873   ◇ K95   ♣ A1087

Four hearts is still some distance away, but if two hearts is all your side can make you are unlikely to buy the contract at that level. Make life difficult for the opponents by bumping the bidding to 3♡.

When the bidding starts with a single raise in a minor, the opener may make a trial bid by calling some other suit. When he bids a major at the two level, in a sequence such as 1◇ – 2◇ – 2♠, the responder is entitled to expect four cards in the suit and may raise, though not above the three level.

At the three level a trial bid may represent merely a stop.

(15)   ♠ AQ10   ♡ 52   ◇ KQJ876   ♣ Q3

After 1◇ – 3◇ you would rebid 3♠, showing your values there. Naturally you hope that partner may now be able to call 3NT.

4.   Support on the second round

We look next at sequences where you are likely to support opener's suit on the second round. It is important to distinguish between sequences that show support and those that merely indicate preference. Suppose partner opens 1♡ and you hold this moderate collection:

(16)   ♠ AQ83   ♡ 74   ◇ 1095   ♣ Q864

You respond 1♠ and partner rebids 2◇. You can be fairly confident that partner holds five hearts but there is no reason to place him with more than four diamonds. You should therefore rebid 2♡. This is described as 'giving preference' to opener's first, and very likely longest, suit. As you see, such a call does not indicate that you hold any positive trump support.

When you return to opener's suit with a jump call, a sequence such as 1♡ – 1♠ – 2◇ – 3♡, this does indicate trump support. You might hold this hand:

(17)   ♠ A10976   ♡ 1063   ◇ K2   ♣ Q84

Such a sequence, 'jump preference' as it is called, invites a game. The opener will pass only when minimum.

Sometimes you are blessed with a hand that is too strong for a direct raise to game. If your hand contains a fair side suit, the best first move is to tell partner of this suit.

(18)   ♠ AJ87   ♡ 92   ◇ AQJ83   ♣ Q6

You are too strong to raise partner's 1♠ directly to 4♠. (Remember that such a raise is often made with defensive intent.) So, you start with a call of 2◇. If partner rebids 2♡ you then jump to 4♠. This sequence, a 'delayed game raise', tells partner that you are full value for a game raise and will welcome any further advance towards a slam.

In a delayed game raise the first suit you name should be of fair quality, preferably KJxxx or better. This assurance will sometimes enable the partnership to reach a slam with the aid of two running 5-card suits and sufficient controls in the other two suits.

When the opener rebids his suit on the second round and the responder raises to game (a sequence such as 1♠ – 2◇ – 2♠ – 4♠), this does not promise 'delayed game raise' values. Should the responder still see chances of a slam, despite his partner's limited rebid, he must cue-bid on the second round (4♣ or 4♡ on this particular sequence).

That brings us to hands of this type:

(19)   ♠ KJ54   ♡ A972   ◇ KQ2   ♣ J6

What should you respond when partner opens 1♠? You have no good side suit for a delayed game raise, but you are too strong for a direct raise to 4♠. The solution is to assign artificial meanings to such otherwise useless responses as 4♣ and 4◇. We will look at two such conventions, Splinter Bids and the Swiss convention, in Chapter 14.

On a really sunny day you may hold a hand where slam is likely even if partner has a near-minimum opening bid. Your first move then will be a jump shift in another suit. Sometimes, when your trump support is exceptional, you may need to 'invent' a jump shift.

(20)   ♠ K7   ♡ AQ1087   ◇ AQ2   ♣ J102

If partner surprises you by opening 1♡ you respond 3◇, intending to bid 4♡ on the next round. Responding 3♣ would not be such a good idea because you have no top card in that suit.

4

Weak or Strong, Partner?

Unless you always play in the same group you will know that there are different ways of playing an opening 1NT. Many British players favour the weak no-trump, generally 12–14. In most other parts of the world the strong no-trump reigns. This shows 15–17 points, or 16–18 for those whose game has an American base.

In the traditional style of the popular Acol system 1NT is 'weak and strong', meaning that you play 12–14 non-vulnerable and 15–17 vulnerable.

As to which is the best scheme, there is no clear answer. Weak throughout may spawn many small gains but will also lead to losing the occasional 800 or 1100. It is therefore favoured more in the tournament world than in rubber bridge, where a big penalty causes a deep scar.

'Weak and strong' still has many followers but it can be a disadvantage if you, in effect, play two different systems according to the vulnerability. That's because the strength of your 1NT opening affects other areas of bidding, such as the 1NT rebid and the need to open with a prepared bid in a minor. Still, there's not much to choose between the methods. If you are happy with what you play at the moment, it's best to stick with it.

The 1NT rebid

Before looking at some sample hands we must discuss the meaning of a 1NT call by the opener on the second round, a sequence such as 1◇ – 1♡ – 1NT. Such a rebid shows the *opposite* strength to that of your 1NT opening. If you play a 15–17 1NT, then a rebid of 1NT shows 12–14; if you play a 12–14 1NT, a rebid of 1NT shows 15–16 (not 17, note). The general idea is that with a flat hand of modest strength you should either open 1NT or plan to rebid in no-trumps.

Playing the weak, 12–14, no-trump

It's time to look at some typical flat hands. In this section we will see
how the weak no-trump (12–14) fares.

(1)   ♠ AJ84   ♡ AQJ2   ◇ J6   ♣ 854

Here, with two suits bare, the old-style player will open 1♠,
intending to rebid 2♡. We don't recommend this style, which too
often leads to a 2♠ contract on a 4–3 or even a 4–2 fit. Stick to your
guns and open 1NT, showing the hand type. If partner has a good
hand he can investigate a 4–4 major-suit fit on the way to game. If
instead he chooses to raise straight to 3NT, he is likely to hold good
values in the minors, if only because he has not investigated the
possibilities of a major-suit contract.

(2)   ♠ Q5   ♡ K93   ◇ KJ1073   ♣ A104

Here you are very happy to open 1NT. The 5-card minor should
provide a good source of tricks.

(3)   ♠ A2   ♡ J9762   ◇ K104   ♣ A84

As a rule, you should not conceal a 5-card major. On this hand,
though, it would not be attractive to have to rebid 2♡ after a start of
1♡ – 1♠. (A 1NT rebid would be strong, remember.) So, open
1NT. You will be surprised how often defenders make a short-suit
lead into the suit that you have concealed.

(4)   ♠ A102   ♡ K1054   ◇ K102   ♣ AJ5

Here you are too strong for a weak no-trump. You have a flat
hand, though, and should aim to tell partner this by rebidding in no-
trumps. So, open 1♡. If partner responds 1♠ you rebid 1NT,
showing 15–16. If instead he responds two of a minor you rebid 2NT,
again showing 15–16 points. Old-fashioned players will sometimes
open a 'prepared club' on this type of hand, intending to rebid 1NT
over 1◇ or 1♠. This is a poor idea when your 4-card suit has any
substance to it.

It is a big advantage of the weak no-trump that you rarely have to resort to such short-suit bids.

Playing the strong, 15–17, no-trump

Now let's look at the same four hands, supposing that we are using a strong no-trump.

(1)   ♠ AJ84   ♡ AQJ2   ◇ J6   ♣ 854

This type of hand is awkward for the strong no-trump. You cannot open 1♡, intending to rebid 2NT over two of a minor, because such a rebid would be 15–16. You must therefore choose between 1♠, intending to rebid 2♡, and a 'short club' bid. Most players would open 1♣ and tell you that they rarely come to any harm by doing so.

(2)   ♠ Q5   ♡ K93   ◇ KJ1073   ♣ A104

No problem here. You open 1◇ and rebid 1NT (12–14) over a major-suit response. Should partner respond 2♣ you can rebid 2◇.

(3)   ♠ A2   ♡ J9762   ◇ K104   ♣ A84

Now you are better placed than when playing the weak no-trump. You can open 1♡ and rebid 1NT over 1♠. Over 2♣ and 2◇ either 2♡ or a raise of partner's suit is acceptable.

(4)   ♠ A102   ♡ K1054   ◇ K102   ♣ AJ5

Who could wish for a more suitable strong no-trump hand?

Responding to 1NT

Tournament players have almost universally adopted transfer responses to 1NT (see Chapter 14) but at rubber bridge such methods are rarely seen, or even allowed. This is the normal scheme for responding to 1NT, whether you play weak or strong:

Pass	No prospect of game and no long suit, except perhaps clubs.
2♣	Stayman (*see below*), asking partner to show a 4-card major.
2◇/2♡/2♠	To play, on a 5-card or longer suit.
2NT	Limit bid; 11–12 opposite a weak no-trump, 8–9 opposite a strong no-trump
3♣/3◇/3♡/3♠	Forcing to game, on a 5-card or longer suit
Game bids	To play
4♣	Gerber convention, asking for aces, (*see* page 91)

After a start such as 1NT – 3♡, the opener will generally bid 3NT when he has only two cards in partner's suit, and will raise to game when he has three-card support.

When responder jumps in a minor suit the opener may show a good suit of his own (since there might still be a fit there), or offer support for partner's minor. Otherwise he will rebid 3NT.

Inexperienced players often make a mistake on hands of this type:

(5)   ♠ AQ6   ♡ 102   ◇ KJ1076   ♣ K43

When partner opens a weak no-trump they respond 3◇. 'Well, the hearts might have been bare,' they say. Such a hand offers very little chance of eleven tricks in a minor-suit game and the correct response is 3NT.

The Stayman Convention

Doubtless you are familiar with the basics of the Stayman convention, where the responder to 1NT bids 2♣, asking you to show a 4-card major. With both majors you rebid 2♡, with neither 2♢. The most common use of the convention is when responder has enough for game and wants to locate a 4–4 fit in a major.

There is more to it than that, though. The player who has bid Stayman may follow with various continuations. Suppose the bidding has started 1NT – 2♣ – 2♡. These options are available to you as responder:

2♠	Mildly invitational, on a 5-card suit. No doubt you would have raised a 2♠ rebid by the opener.
2NT	Limit bid. It may be assumed that you have 4 spades, since otherwise you would have raised to 2NT directly.
3♣	Weak hand with long clubs.
3♢	An encouraging call, since with a weak hand you could have bid 2♢ initially.
3♡	A raise of partner's 4-card major is invitational.
3♠	Non-forcing game try on at least a 5-card suit.
3NT	To play, but you should have four spades; partner may correct to 4♠ if he holds both majors.

As you see, 2♣ is used almost as a relay bid. A call such as 3♠ by responder has different meanings, according to whether it is bid directly or via Stayman.

Suppose partner opens a 12–14 1NT and you hold this hand:

(6)   ♠ AQ10762   ♡ K3   ◇ J63   ♣ 105

Here you want to invite a spade game. An immediate response of
3♠ would be forcing to game, so you start with a Stayman 2♣. Over
a 2◇ or 2♡ response you will jump to 3♠, non-forcing but invitational.

You might instead hold this responding hand:

(7)   ♠ 104   ♡ KQ52   ◇ 63   ♣ AQ852

You start with 2♣, looking for a heart fit. If partner disappoints
with a 2◇ or 2♠ rebid, you continue with 2NT, non-forcing but
inviting partner to bid 3NT.

Rebids of 2NT and 3NT

We saw earlier that the strength of a 1NT rebid depended on
whether a 1NT opening would have been weak or strong. Rebids of
2NT and 3NT do not vary in this way. This is the general scheme:

When partner responds at the one level

1◇ – 1♡ – 2NT	17–18 points.
1♣ – 1♠ – 3NT	about 19 points.

When partner responds at the two level

1♠ – 2♣ – 2NT	15–16 points.
1♡ – 2♣ – 3NT	17–19 points.

Suppose you are dealt this hand:

(8)   ♠ KQ5   ♡ A108   ◇ AQ832   ♣ 105

Playing a weak no-trump, you open 1◇. If partner responds 1♡
or 1♠ you may either raise him or express your general values by
rebidding 1NT. If instead he responds 2♣ you are dead centre for a
rebid of 2NT, showing a balanced hand in the 15–16 range. Playing

a strong no-trump you would settle matters at once by opening 1NT.

(9)   ♠ AJ8   ♡ A10   ♢ KQ742   ♣ KJ6

After 1♢ – 1♡, or 1♢ – 1♠, you would rebid 2NT, showing around 17–18 points. After 1♢ – 2♣ you are worth 3NT. The logic behind this, of course, is that partner shows more strength when he responds at the two level.

5

The Opener Limits his Hand

When the bidding starts with two suit bids, such as 1♢ – 1♠, very little is known about the strengths of the two hands. The opener might hold a shapely 10 points or perhaps a flat 19-count. The responder may have summoned a response on some feeble 5-count or he may hold a massive two-suiter and be thinking of a slam.

On the second round of bidding both players will attempt to give some picture of their strength and in this chapter we look at the situation from the opener's point of view. We saw in Chapter 3 how the opener deals with flat hands. Here we look at distributional hands. The subject is tackled in this order:

1. The opener is near minimum.
2. The opener has some values to spare.
3. The opener has enough for game.

1. The opener is near minimum

When the opener has a distributional hand that is near a minimum, usually 12 to 14 points, he has three options – he may rebid his suit, give partner a single raise, or bid a new suit.

(1)   ♠ AKJ964   ♡ J842   ♢ 5   ♣ Q5

You open 1♠ and partner responds 2♣ or 2♢. It would be ill-advised to rebid 2♡. You opened the hand because of the good spade suit and 2♠ is the more descriptive rebid. Also, a rebid of your first suit indicates a somewhat minimum hand. To call a new suit, 2♡, does not limit your hand in the same way.

(2)   ♠ A105   ♡ 3   ♢ AQ973   ♣ Q762

You open 1◇ and partner says 1♠. You have a minimum hand and must choose between showing your second suit and raising partner's spades. On such occasions prefer to raise partner's suit. Not only is this more likely to be helpful to partner, it also limits your hand, telling him that you have a near minimum. A rebid of 2♣, a new suit, would not limit your hand in this way.

2. The opener has values to spare

When the opener has around 15–18 points, or equivalent distributional values, he will usually be too strong for a simple rebid of his suit or a single raise of partner's suit. He must find some other move.

(3)　　♠ A3　　♡ 106　　◇ AQJ752　　♣ KQ8

You start with 1◇ and partner responds 1♠. No problem here, you rebid 3◇. This is non-forcing but indicates a hand of around 16 points. If this does not inspire partner to seek a game somewhere he may pass. If instead he makes some advance – 3♡ or perhaps 3♠, a rebid of his suit – this will be forcing to game.

(4)　　♠ 2　　♡ AK108642　　◇ A4　　♣ J75

After 1♡ – 1♠ you rebid 3♡. As you see, such a jump rebid is not just a matter of counting points.

When you have primary support for partner's major, and the values for a game try, you give a double raise.

(5)　　♠ A1087　　♡ KQ872　　◇ A5　　♣ K6

After 1♡ – 1♠ you are happy to raise to 3♠. Partner is free to pass. Should he instead continue with a call such as 4♣, this will be a cue bid, showing a control in that suit and suggesting a slam.

It is a common fault to give a double raise on hands of this type:

(6)   ♠ J852   ♡ AQ9765   ♢ –   ♣ KJ9

After 1♡ – 1♠ it is perfectly safe to rebid just 2♠. The effect of any more energetic move would be to propel yourself towards a slam with insufficient power between the two hands and, very likely, an inadequate trump suit.

That still leaves many hands where you will have to make a call in a new suit. Calls which introduce a new suit leave the strength of the hand relatively undefined.

(7)   ♠ A5   ♡ AQJ76   ♢ KQJ4   ♣ 52

You open 1♡ and partner responds 1♠ or 2♣. You rebid 2♢, showing your distribution but leaving partner in the dark as to whether you hold 11 points or 17. On this type of hand it is usually the responder who will make the first limit bid. If, for example, he now limits his hand with a rebid of 2♠, you will indicate your additional values here by raising to 3♠.

No doubt you have heard players speak of a 'reverse'. This occurs when opener rebids at the two level in a higher suit than that of the opening bid, for example 1♢ – 1♠ – 2♡. If responder, on some miserable 6-count, prefers your longer suit he will now have to bid 3♢. Since the bidding will often be carried to the three level in this way, it follows that you need extra values to reverse, usually at least 16 points.

(8)   ♠ J4   ♡ AKJ6   ♢ AK1054   ♣ J9

Here you do have the values to reverse. You open 1♢, intending to rebid 2♡ over 1♠. If instead of ♡A you held a small heart, you would still open 1♢ but then, lacking the values for a reverse, you would have to rebid 2♢. Note that the first-bid suit in a reverse is *always* longer than the second.

A reverse is non-forcing opposite a one-level response. Opposite a two-level response it is, in effect, forcing to game, since the minimum values held will be something like 16 points facing 10.

Some confusion may arise on sequences of this type, where there has been intervention:

West	*North*	*East*	*South*
1♣	1♠	2◇	Pass
2♡			

Does West show reversing values or not? There is no reason to assume so. West has made the cheapest bid possible and was doubtless intending to rebid just 1♡ over a response of 1◇.

3.   The opener has enough for game

Since there have been some recent changes of style concerning the opener's rebid facing a two-level response, we will consider separately the situations facing one-level and two-level responses.

When partner has responded at the one level

Sometimes the mere fact that responder has found a one-level response is enough to spur the opener towards game.

(9)   ♠ AJ2   ♡ AQ109862   ◇ AQ   ♣ 4

You open 1♡ and partner responds 1♠. What now? You are worth 4♡. Such a call implies some support for partner's spades, since otherwise you would doubtless have opened a strong 2♡.

(10)   ♠ AQ10   ♡ 8   ◇ AKJ942   ♣ AJ5

Here, after 1◇ – 1♡, you are too good for a non-forcing 3◇. The most practical bid is 3NT. Partner should bear in mind that this rebid may be based on an excellent diamond suit. He should *not* revert to 4♡ on such as six miserable hearts to the king.

Next we must look at hands where you have excellent support for responder's suit, enough to insist on a game contract at least.

(11)   ♠ AQ92   ♡ J4   ◇ AKJ87   ♣ K2

After 1◇ – 1♠, you raise to 4♠. Sometimes you hear of missed slams after this sequence with the responder saying 'I took your 4♠ as a shut-out, partner'. This is not right, of course. If you bid game when all partner has indicated to you is a 4-card spade suit and around 6 points, it is obvious that you have a fine hand.

When your hand is even stronger you will want to give partner a hint that slam may be possible.

(12)   ♠ AQ92   ♡ 4   ◇ AKJ873   ♣ AJ

When your 1◇ opening attracts a 1♠ response you realise that partner will need very little for a slam to be on. You rebid 4♣, a double jump, showing a control in clubs and excellent spade support. Some players use such a leap to show specifically a shortage in the suit called. (*See* Splinter Bid in Chapter 14.)

Finally there are hands where the opener has a powerful hand with two suits of his own. Since a sequence such as 1♡ – 1♠ – 2◇ is non-forcing there comes a time when you have to rebid 3◇, to make sure that partner bids again.

(13)   ♠ A2   ♡ AKJ76   ◇ AQ1092   ♣ 5

Here you would be apprehensive if partner let the bidding die after 1♡ – 1♠ – 2◇. Although you can't be absolutely certain that game is on, you must take the bold course of rebidding 3◇, forcing to game.

Such a rebid is often made when you have a good fit for responder's suit and are trying to paint as accurate a picture as possible in case a slam is on.

(14)   ♠ A1072   ♡ AK1093   ◇ AQ4   ♣ 2

After 1♡ – 1♠ you will not want to play any lower than 4♠. If you make such a bid directly, though, partner will be in the dark as to your minor-suit holdings. Rebid 3◇ instead and go to 4♠ on the next round. Now if partner has values to spare he will be better placed to judge the slam prospects. For example, he will realise that the diamond king is a valuable card; the club king may be worthless.

When partner has responded at the two level

A two-level response suggests at least 10 points and the chances are greater that the opener will want to insist on game. Traditionally a sequence such as 1♠ – 2♣ – 2◇ is non-forcing. However, since the opener might hold a very fair hand – anything just short of a 3◇ rebid, which would be game-forcing – it was rare for the 2◇ rebid to be passed out. Many modern bidders have carried this a stage further, making a new suit by the opener *forcing* after a two-level response.

Although you must check this approach with any new partner, such an agreement certainly makes the game easier. Let's see some examples of the method.

(15)   ♠ AQJ92   ♡ KQ52   ◇ A3   ♣ J7

The bidding starts 1♠ – 2◇. If 2♡ is non-forcing you cannot risk it and must rebid 3♡. Now, though, responder has no idea whether you hold four hearts or five. He may have to guess which game to bid. The auction will breathe more easily if the new-suit bid of 2♡ is treated as forcing.

(16)   ♠ AK965   ♡ AJ102   ◇ K95   ♣ 6

Here, after the same start of 1♠ – 2◇, you have three messages to pass to partner: you are strong, you have a heart suit, and you have diamond support. Again it will be easier to paint a full picture if you can start with a 2♡ rebid, confident that it will not be passed.

The same may be said of a 2NT rebid after a two-level response. Since this normally indicates 15–16 points and partner has suggested around 10 or more, surely it is a good idea to make the 2NT rebid forcing? This is becoming normal practice in the tournament world; again you must check with your partner what his views are on the matter.

Earlier in this section we mentioned that a jump rebid opposite a one-level response was non-forcing. Opposite a two-level response such a rebid is forcing.

    (17)   ♠ AKJ874   ♡ 62   ◇ AJ2   ♣ K10

If your 1♠ opening attracts a 2♣ or 2◇ response you will rebid 3♠, which is now forcing. Once more this makes good sense since the combined values figure to be 16 opposite 10, at least. Clearly it would be very space-consuming if such a rebid were not forcing and you had to rebid 4♠ instead. If the opener does in fact follow a sequence such as 1♠ – 2◇ – 4♠ he indicates a hand worth game, with very good spades but little of interest outside.

A non-jump rebid at the three level, a sequence such as 1♠ – 2♡ – 3♣, is known as a 'high reverse' and is game-forcing. Usually the second suit will contain at least four cards but such a bid may be used to herald support for partner.

    (18)   ♠ 2   ♡ KQJ87   ◇ AQ102   ♣ AJ4

After 1♡ – 2◇ you could raise to 4◇, which would be forcing, but this would give partner little idea of your holdings in the black suits. It is more descriptive to rebid 3♣, then support diamonds strongly on the next round. Among other things, this will give partner a picture of your singleton spade, quietening his fears when he holds two or three small cards in this suit.

6

Responder Limits his Hand

By the time the responder makes his second call he will generally have a fair idea of the level at which the contract should be played. Unless the auction has started with three bids in different suits, such as 1♡ – 1♠ – 2♣, one or other player will already have made a limit bid. Whether or not this is the case, the responder's second call is likely to be a limit bid of some sort.

We will look at his action under these categories:

1. Responder signs off.
2. Responder makes a game try.
3. Responder heads for game.
4. Responder asks for more information.

The responder signs off

When the opener has made a limit bid himself (perhaps 1◇ – 1♠ – 2◇, or 1♣ – 1♡ – 2♡) responder will simply pass when there are no game prospects. When you are weak it is a mistake to fight against the opener's suit.

(1)   ♠ Q10874   ♡ KJ42   ◇ 6   ♣ 1093

After 1◇ – 1♠ – 2◇ it is unwise to fight on with 2♡ and you should pass. A second-round call of 2♡ would not be forcing, in traditional methods, but it does have to cover many hands that are stronger than this. At any rate, the opener will feel entitled to carry on bidding when his hand is better than it might be.

The same is true when you have a weak hand with, say, six spades and only one diamond. After 1◇ – 1♠ – 2◇ you should be inclined to call it a day, rather than press the claims of your spade suit. The time to rebid your suit is when your hand is almost worth a game try.

(2)　　♠ AQ9862　　♡ KJ4　　♢ 65　　♣ 82

Here, after 1♢ – 1♠ – 2♢, you would have no second thoughts about continuing with 2♠. If partner then gave you a nudge with 3♠ you would advance to game.

Perhaps the most common form of responder's sign-off is when he gives simple preference to the opener's first suit.

(3)　　♠ AQ76　　♡ 92　　♢ Q2　　♣ 97542

After 1♡ – 1♠ – 2♢ you have nothing constructive to say and must bid a dutiful 2♡, giving preference to partner's first suit. Partner's 2♢ rebid covers a wide range, of course, and it will be no surprise if he makes some further move towards game.

The responder makes a game try

When responder makes a limit bid of 2NT on the second round he suggests around 10–12 points, though occasionally he may hold less. The bottom end is slightly lower than for a 2NT response on the first round because of hands like this:

(4)　　♠ A1072　　♡ 8　　♢ Q76　　♣ K10432

After 1♡ – 1♠ – 2♢ you can hardly pass because the opener may hold 16 points or so. You must say 2NT, giving partner another chance to speak.

Another common form of game try is a limit bid in one of the opener's suits:

(5)　　♠ 87　　♡ A72　　♢ J52　　♣ AQ943

After 1♡ – 2♣ – 2♢ you give jump preference to 3♡. This is non-forcing but invitational; you would make the same call if opener had rebid 2♡.

Finally there are the hands where you wish to invite game in your own suit.

(6)   ♠ A3   ♡ KQJ762   ◇ J4   ♣ 1086

After 1◇ – 1♡ – 2♣ you jump to 3♡, suggesting around 10–11 points and a good suit.

The responder heads for game

On many strongish responding hands you will simply bid some game or other on the second round. When you have enough for game but still cannot tell the best denomination, various forcing moves are available.

(7)   ♠ AQ87   ♡ AK632   ◇ 6   ♣ 986

After 1◇ – 1♡ – 2◇ you may bid 2♠, introducing your spade suit. This 'responder's reverse' is forcing for one round. On this occasion you have no intention of letting the bidding die below game level.

A new suit at the three level is also forcing.

(8)   ♠ A2   ♡ 4   ◇ AQJ82   ♣ Q10763

After 1♡ – 2◇ – 2♡ you proceed naturally with 3♣. If partner gives you preference to 3◇ you will bid 3♠, hoping that partner has some help for you in spades and can call 3NT.

Sometimes responder must 'invent' a bid on a suit of less than four cards.

(9)   ♠ 87   ♡ AQ1076   ◇ K74   ♣ AJ4

After 1◇ – 1♡ – 2◇ you are much too strong for a non-forcing 3◇. It would be undisciplined to bid 3NT with two small spades, so the best move is 3♣. Partner will know what to do if he has the spades well stopped, or if he has some support for your hearts. If instead he gives unwelcome support to your clubs, no damage is done; you will simply revert to diamonds.

The responder seeks more information

So far responder has been able to continue the auction by using bids that are more or less natural. There are many hands, though, for which no natural bid is satisfactory. Suppose you hold this collection:

(10)   ♠ AQ873   ♡ K4   ◇ 872   ♣ A65

If the bidding starts 1♡ – 1♠ – 2♣, no natural call is remotely satisfactory for responder. You can hardly bid 3NT without a diamond stop; and a call such as 3♠ would be non-forcing, suggesting fewer points and a better spade suit. The answer to this and many similar situations is to make an artificial bid in the *fourth suit*, here 2◇. Such a call, known as 'fourth suit forcing', shows that you have at least game-try values and would like partner to continue describing his hand. It doesn't promise anything at all in the suit artificially called; indeed if you had values there you would probably have bid no-trumps yourself.

This would be a typical auction involving the hand above:

West	East	West	East
♠6	♠AQ873	1♡	1♠
♡AQ1065	♡K4	2♣	2◇
◇A103	◇872	2NT	3NT
♣K972	♣A65	End	

Now give West a slightly different hand:

West	East	West	East
♠64	♠AQ873	1♡	1♠
♡AQJ65	♡K4	2♣	2◇
◇103	◇872	2♡	4♡
♣KQ72	♣A65	End	

East is able to choose the best game in both cases.

One important question to settle with your partner is how far a fourth-suit bid should be forcing. The simplest idea is that if the opener rebids at the two level, responder may pass. If the opener rebids at the three level, or if responder himself makes any call following his fourth-suit bid, then the bidding must proceed to game.

Suppose you hold:

(11)   ♠ KJ64   ♡ A102   ◇ AQ873   ♣ 9

The bidding starts 1◇ – 1♡ – 1♠, then your partner produces a fourth-suit 2♣. What should you say? A call of 2♡ would be non-forcing and would nowhere near do justice to your hand. Remember that partner has at least game-try values and is very likely to have five hearts too. Clearly, you must bid 3♡.

Sometimes it is necessary for responder to bid the fourth suit even though he has a primary fit for one of opener's suits.

(12)   ♠ AJ762   ♡ 7   ◇ A53   ♣ K1084

After 1♡ – 1♠ – 2♣ you are too strong for a non-forcing raise to 3♣. You should temporise with a fourth-suit call of 2◇, then bid 3♣ on the next round. This call then becomes forcing. This is a valuable use of the fourth suit – as a type of relay, giving you forcing and non-forcing variants of a subsequent call.

The same principle applies here:

(13)   ♠ AQ8742   ♡ J   ◇ 1083   ♣ AQ2

The bidding starts 1♡ – 1♠ – 2♣. A call of 3♠ now would be a non-forcing limit bid. You therefore bid 2◇, intending to make a (forcing) 3♠ call on the next round.

Sometimes the opener can make a fourth suit bid.

(14)   ♠ J3   ♡ AKJ76   ◇ A75   ♣ 982

After 1♡ – 1♠ – 2♡ – 3♣ the best game might yet be in hearts, spades or no-trumps. The opener does best to seek further information by bidding the fourth suit, here 3◇.

7

Strong Opening Hands

In most natural systems there are three different ways of expressing a big hand – 2NT, an Acol Two, and the 2♣ opening. We look at these in turn.

The 2NT opening

The usual standard is 20–22, but the bid is sometimes made on slightly less, especially when a 5-card suit is held. As a rule, it is unwise to open 1NT with a 5-card major, but 2NT is easily the best opening on a hand such as:

(1)   ♠ A10   ♡ AQJ85   ◇ AJ9   ♣ K86

The advantage is not so much that 1♡ might be passed out when there is a game on; there are other considerations in favour of 2NT. The hand will probably be played the right way up, with the strong hand concealed; opponents will not suspect the good heart suit. Also, when partner has a good hand himself a 2NT opening will make it easier for him to visualise a slam.

Give yourself a couple of points more.

(2)   ♠ KJ4   ♡ AK1076   ◇ AJ   ♣ AJ7

Now an opening 1♡ is out of the question; you are too strong. An Acol 2♡, perhaps? Many players would choose this call, then sit wondering what to do when partner responds 2NT. Eventually they would rebid a strangled 3NT, too high when partner has next to nothing. Also, they would play the contract the wrong way round. The only sensible opening is 2NT, playing there when partner is very weak.

Responding to 2NT

In the tournament world transfer responses are almost universal (*see* Chapter 14). The traditional responses, used for rubber bridge, follow this scheme:

3♣	Baron, after which both players bid 4-card suits until 3NT is reached.
3◇/3♡/3♠	A suit of at least 5 cards, forcing to game.
Game bids	To play
4♣	Gerber, asking for aces, (*see* page 91)
4NT	Limit bid, inviting 6NT

The main advantage of the Baron 3♣ response, as compared to a Stayman 3♣, is that 4–4 fits in a minor suit may be located.

West	*East*
♠AJ	♠Q952
♡AJ74	♡3
◇KQ95	◇A1063
♣AQ5	♣K864

If you play Stayman responses the bidding is likely to go:

West	*East*
2NT	3♣
3♡	3♠
3NT	?

It would be unsound for East to make any further move.

Playing the Baron style, the slam is easy to reach:

West	East
2NT	3♣
3◇	3♠
3NT	4◇
6◇	End

Acol two bids

In traditional Acol opening calls of 2◇, 2♡ and 2♠ express powerful hands, too good for an opening bid of one. In the old phrase, such an opening denotes a hand of power and quality. Writers often use the phrase '8 playing tricks', but this accounts for only one type. Compare these two hands:

(3)   ♠ KQJ974   ♡ A8   ◇ AQJ5   ♣ 5

(4)   ♠ AKJ83   ♡ 7   ◇ AQJ96   ♣ A4

Hand (3) is a minimum two bid, just about worth 8 playing tricks. On (4) you cannot count the playing tricks until you know about the fit – or absence of a fit – but you certainly don't want to be left in 1♠, so you open 2♠.

Except when the responding hand is a complete 'stinker', Acol two bids are forcing to the level of three in the suit opened. The weakness response, according to tradition, is 2NT (though there is something to be said for Herbert responses – see Chapter 14).

When you make a positive response you should not, as a rule, name a suit in which you lack both ace and king. Suppose partner opens 2♡ and you are lucky enough to hold:

(5)   ♠ K7   ♡ 93   ◇ AQ64   ♣ Q10852

If you wish to give a positive, make it 3◇ rather than 3♣. The opener will have a strong suit or suits of his own and will not be interested in the queen-high clubs. Indeed there are many players who would keep the bidding low by responding 2NT, allowing partner to define his hand. This doesn't stop you from springing to life later.

As for raising an Acol two, trump support of three small or Qx is generally sufficient. A double raise, such as 2♡ – 4♡, suggests fair values (about 8–10 points) but no ace. A raise to three is forcing and may be the first move on a good hand. Suppose partner opens 2♠ and you hold one of these hands:

(6)	♠Q1065	(7)	♠Q87	(8)	♠K8
	♡J872		♡K652		♡AJ76
	◇1092		◇J2		◇Q932
	♣J2		♣Q1092		♣875

On (6) you want to head for an eventual 4♠ but not to encourage partner to hit the slam trail. You start with a 2NT response (forcing, of course); if partner makes some three-level rebid, you go to 4♠ then. Hand (7) is better; you hold enough to raise 2♠ directly to 4♠. Hand (8) represents a fair chance of a slam opposite a 2♠ opening. Your first response is 3♠, a stronger call than 4♠; partner may then make a cue bid, initiating slam investigations.

The 2♣ opener

As most of us learnt on our mother's knee, the only 2♣ sequence that may stop short of game is 2♣ – 2◇ – 2NT. It follows that this is the right sequence to use on many flattish 23-counts that contain a 5-card major. To rebid 2♡ or 2♠ instead would commit your side to game. After 2♣ – 2◇ – 2NT, the responses are the same as those facing a 2NT opening. 3♣ should again be Baron (or Stayman).

The modern tendency is to use the weakness response of 2◇ on many quite useful hands. This allows the opener to express his type economically, the idea being that the responder will then know in what direction to advance.

Here are a couple of typical sequences, starting with a 2♣ opening:

West	East	West	East
♠AK4	♠J73	2♣	2◇
♡AKQ87	♡104	2♡	3♣
◇AJ105	◇842	3◇	3♡
♣K	♣Q10952	3NT	End

West describes his wonderful hand, then rightly leaves any move towards a slam to his partner. When dummy comes down West will see that game is quite high enough.

West	East	West	East
♠KQ87	♠A93	2♣	2NT
♡AJ92	♡Q103	3NT	6NT
◇AK4	◇QJ82	End	
♣AQ	♣J95		

East has enough for a positive response but no good suit to call; he therefore makes his positive bid in no-trumps. West, with a bare 23 points, rebids just 3NT. East judges that the combined assets should offer good play for a small slam and so it proves. If the heart finesse is right there are twelve easy tricks. If the heart finesse loses, declarer will have several extra chances in the black suits.

8

Pre-emptive Openings

An opening bid of three shows a weak hand with a long suit, normally of seven cards. The idea, of course, is to make life difficult for the opponents, who probably hold most of the high cards. Since the dawn of time bridge books have advocated the Rule of 500, suggesting that you should not open with a three bid unless you have a reasonable prospect of holding the loss to 500 opposite a balanced yarborough. There is more to it than that as most players nowadays have realised.

How would you rate this hand as an opening pre-empt?

(1)　　　♠ J104　　♡ 75　　♢ 8　　♣ KJ108532

It represents a standard three club opening, when non-vulnerable. With clubs as trumps you expect to make at least five tricks; if you were defending you would scarcely expect to make any. That is one measure of a hand's suitability for a pre-emptive opening: it is worth much more in attack than in defence. Such a hand is worth a three bid even if the potential loss is more than the proverbial 500. If you were vulnerable, though, the possible penalty would be too great; you would have to pass.

(2)　　　♠ A1052　　♡ 86　　♢ –　　♣ K976432

Here we see the other side of the coin, a hand that is quite unsuitable for a pre-emptive opening. Why is that? One reason is that if partner has no fit for either black suit you may lose a fortune, perhaps not even in a good cause. Another is that when partner does have a fit for you, perhaps a hand such as ♠Kx ♡KQx ♢Jxxx ♣AJxx, he won't dream that game or slam may be lay-down. Finally, you have a 4-card major on the side and may miss a fit there if you open 3♣. So, you see that it is not that the hand is too weak or too strong, just that it is the wrong type for pre-emptive action.

Possession of a 4-card major is no bar to a three opening if the hand is otherwise suitable.

    (3)   ♠ K932   ♡ 8   ♢ 5   ♣ QJ109763

Here you have five tricks or so if you play the hand, scarcely a single trick in defence – ideal for pre-emptive action and you can open 3♣ at any vulnerability. Does such an opening risk missing a game in spades? Of course it does. Once in a blue moon.

Pre-empts in the third position

When you are sitting in the third seat and the auction starts with two passes should your three bids be weak or strong? The answer is . . . yes! Sometimes they should be very weak, sometimes relatively strong.

Suppose first that you are non-vulnerable and have a very weak type:

    (4)   ♠ J87   ♡ 104   ♢ Q1087643   ♣ 9

With two passed hands in front of you it does not take a clairvoyant to place the fourth player with a big hand. Annoy him by opening 3♢. Most players use a double for take-out anyway, so you are unlikely to be caught for a large number. Even if you are, it will almost certainly be in a good cause.

Now suppose that there have been two passes and you hold this collection:

    (5)   ♠ Q5   ♡ 8   ♢ AKJ9762   ♣ J103

Again you should open 3♢. You would be much too strong for such action in the first or second seat, but here the risk of missing anything is made much smaller by the fact that partner has passed. Also, it is likely that the fourth player has some length in the majors and your opening will make it harder for him to express this. Let the opponents guess which type of pre-empt you have.

Pre-empts in fourth position

Obviously you would not open with a very weak pre-empt in fourth seat. A simpler way to ensure silence on the part of the opposition is to pass. That doesn't mean that a pre-empt in fourth seat should show particularly good values. It should indicate the type of hand where you feel you can grab a part score, but are worried that the opponents may have a fit somewhere themselves.

    (6)   ♠ Q   ♡ 97   ◇ AQJ1062   ♣ KJ92

    To open 1◇ would invite competition in the majors. A call of 3◇ has a reasonable chance of holding the field.

Responding to pre-empts

There are times when you have to take defensive action. Suppose the man opposite opens 3♠ and you hold;

    (7)   ♠ K42   ♡ 9842   ◇ Q10953   ♣ 3

You are clearly outgunned, but four spades doubled – and it may not be – will not be too expensive. So, maintain course by raising to 4♠.

You would make the same response on this hand:

    (8)   ♠ 8   ♡ AK82   ◇ AQ64   ♣ KQ53

Here you expect to make 4♠. (In case we need to say it, 3NT would not be a good idea. Dummy's spades would be useless and you would probably go three or four down.)

What does it mean when you respond in a different suit? That depends on whether the opening is in a minor or a major. A start such as 3♣ – 3♡ indicates that responder has a good hand, probably with at least 6 hearts. The call is forcing for the present and the opener should support hearts if at all possible.

The situation is different when partner has opened three of a major. Suppose the bidding starts 3♠ – 4♣. Far more often than not, this will mean interest in a spade slam.

It may well be a 'cue bid' (*see* Chapter 9), showing a good spade fit, the ace of clubs and slam interest. The opener will now sign off in 4♠ if his pre-empt is relatively weak. With a fair hand he will make some other move. Here is a typical auction:

West	East	West	East
♠AQ87652	♠K4	3♠	4♣
♡94	♡AJ1052	4◇	6♠
◇K52	◇AQ6	End	
♣8	♣AJ7		

East suggests a spade slam by cue-bidding in clubs. (Generally you choose the lowest suit where you hold a top control.) West has the perfect hand for co-operating in a slam venture, good trumps and a useful high card outside. Spades have already been agreed as trumps, so his 4◇ call is another cue bid, showing a control of some sort. This is enough for East, who leaps straight to six. If West's hand had been weaker, say with ◇J instead of ◇K, he would have signed off in 4♠, ending the auction. This last example implies, it is true, a more respectful attitude to three bids than exists in the tournament world. Rubber bridge players, in general, do not favour very weak pre-empts.

Defending against Pre-empts

On most occasions the best defence against opening pre-empts is a simple take-out double. It wastes no space and leaves all other calls, in particular 3NT, to have a natural meaning. It does mean that you lose the chance to make an immediate penalty double, but this is not a serious loss. If you pass, holding good trumps over the opener, partner may re-open with a double. If instead you have a strong all-round hand, you will score just as well by playing in 3NT.

The next question is how strong you need to be to enter over a pre-empt. In the second seat you need to be about a king stronger than for a minimum double at the one-level. Suppose the first player has opened 3◇ and you sit over him with this hand:

(9)   ♠ KQ93   ♡ AJ842   ◇ 87   ♣ A4

You should enter with a double. You *might* find a giant hand sitting over you and run into a heavy penalty. You could spend a lifetime worrying about this sort of thing, though. It's not clever to escape two penalties and miss half a dozen good contracts.

Neither should you be worried that partner will respond in clubs. He will realise that you are more likely to be interested in the majors. If he bids 4♣ or 5♣ he will have a fair suit of his own.

When you have a one-suited hand you must balance the risk of suffering a big penalty against the prospect of making a game your way. Suppose you hear a 3♣ opening on your right and you hold this hand:

    (10)   ♠ AQJ87   ♡ 5   ◇ AK102   ♣ J83

Of course it is somewhat dangerous to enter with 3♠ but it is even more dangerous to pass, possibly missing a good game your way.

When a three-bid is followed by two passes you can enter with slightly less in the fourth seat than you would need in the second seat. Don't overdo this, though, since the third player may have passed on a good hand if he has no trump fit with the opener.

    (11)   ♠ AJ932   ♡ K1053   ◇ Q74   ♣ 9

After 3♣ – Pass – Pass this hand is minimum for a double, but most good players would risk it. Move a small heart into the diamond suit and the scales would topple; you would probably pass.

9

Slam Bidding

An important part of good slam bidding is to make the slam suggestion *before* the bidding has passed the game level. We have already looked at one way you can do this – by making a jump-shift response to partner's opening bid. This in itself airs the possibility of a slam; when your jump shift was something of a minimum you can subsequently settle in some game contract, leaving partner to make any further running.

In this chapter we look at another way to invite a slam: the control-showing cue bid. Here is an example of such a call.

West	East	West	East
♠AKJ1063	♠Q954	1♠	3♠
♡84	♡K106	4♣	4♠
◇J	◇KQ105	End	
♣AK104	♣J3		

When West hears a double raise it seems quite possible that the two hands will provide a play for twelve tricks. Since spades have been agreed as trumps, and any further move over 3♠ will carry the auction to game (at least), West's 4♣ is a *cue bid*. It carries these messages:

(a) 'I have the strength to consider a slam.'

(b) 'I have the ace or king (sometimes a singleton or void) in clubs.'

On the present occasion East's hand is short of controls, quite unsuitable for slam purposes. He indicates this by signing off in 4♠ and the partnership comes safely to rest.

See how hopeless it would have been for West to introduce Blackwood instead, as many players would. The resultant 5♠ contract might well go down.

Let's see an example where the partner of the cue-bidder does want to cooperate in a slam venture.

West	East	West	East
♠AJ87	♠KQ1054	1♡	1♠
♡AQJ1076	♡K3	3♠	4♣
♢4	♢J87	4♢	4♡
♣Q5	♣A106	4NT	5♢
		6♠	End

East suggests a slam with his 4♣ call. West is happy to join in the action and cue-bids 4♢, an example of making such a call on a singleton. East's 4♡ cue bid solidifies West's suit, making him confident that the playing strength is present for a slam. A Blackwood call indicates that there is an ace missing and West pulls down the shutters at the six level.

Note that it is not a good idea to cue-bid a singleton or void in partner's main suit; that is usually the last holding that will prove useful. In the auction above, it was important for West to know that the 4♡ cue bid would be based on a top honour.

Sometimes aces and kings are useless in one suit, priceless in another. Cue-bidding can help you find out which. Look at these two auctions:

West	East	West	East
♠AQJ1084	♠K92	2♠	3♠
♡QJ7	♡AK83	4♣	4♡
♢AKQ10	♢762	5♢	5♡
♣–	♣1053	5NT	6♣
		7♠	End

East cue-bids twice in hearts, plugging West's gaps in that department. West's 5NT call asks how many of the three top trumps his partner holds (*see* Grand Slam Try, Chapter 14). When East admits to the missing trump honour, West bids the grand with confidence.

See what happens when East has the same high-card strength but it is distributed less helpfully.

West	East	West	East
♠AQJ1084	♠K92	2♠	3♠
♡QJ7	♡1053	4♣	4♠
◇AKQ10	◇762	End	
♣–	♣AK83		

East shuts up shop in 4♠ at his second turn, knowing that his only side-suit controls are placed opposite a shortage. Even if East takes an optimistic view and carries the bidding to the five-level with a 5♣ cue bid at his second turn, the bidding will then go 5◇ – 5♠ and the partnership will stop at a reasonably safe level.

The familiar Blackwood 4NT convention asks how many aces partner holds, the traditional responses being:

5♣	0 or 4 aces
5◇	1 ace
5♡	2 aces
5♠	3 aces

This is an inefficient set of responses and we describe a much better scheme (Roman Key Card Blackwood) in Chapter 14. Whatever responses you play, though, it is important to know *when* you should use Blackwood. You can see how useless Blackwood would have been in the two cue-bid auctions we looked at a moment ago. You should use Blackwood only when these conditions are satisfied:

(a)   The playing strength is there for a slam;

(b)   The partnership has at least second-round control of every suit;

(c)   A disappointing response will not carry you past the safe level in your trump suit;

(d)   You will know what to do after the Blackwood response.

Here is an example of correct usage:

West	East	West	East
♠AKJ87	♠63	1♠	2♡
♡K1094	♡AQJ832	3♡	4♣
◇6	◇Q107	4NT	5♡
♣J95	♣A3	6♡	End

West's hand is good in the context of his single raise; when his partner makes a slam suggestion he can be confident that the combined playing strength will be adequate for twelve tricks. Partner's club cue bid also tells him that every side suit is under at least second-round control. West launches the old Black and, as you see, the eventual six hearts is a fine contract. Declarer will play on spades to establish a discard for his club loser.

Responding to Blackwood with a void

An unexpected void, not in the 4NT bidder's main side suit, can be a big asset, but it is not sound to treat it as equivalent to an ace in your Blackwood response. When the responder has one ace and what may be a critical void he may by-pass the standard response and leap to the six level. If his void is in a suit below the trump suit he bids six of that suit, otherwise six of the trump suit. For example:

West	West	East
♠AK964	1♠	2◇
♡–	3◇	4NT
◇KQ62	?	
♣10854		

It is charitable to assume that East holds at least second-round control of clubs (and hearts). South leaps to 6◇ to express one ace and a void – obviously a void in hearts, because if the hearts and clubs were reversed South would bid 6♣.

5NT to play

It can happen occasionally that the response to 4NT indicates that two aces are missing but the level is already beyond five of the intended suit. A gadget exists to allow the partnership to come to rest in 5NT. The Blackwood caller bids five of a completely new suit and responder must now bid 5NT, where the bidding rests. Good luck to them!

Responding to Blackwood when opponents intervene

Suppose that the bidding begins in this fashion:

South	West	North	East
1♡	2◇	3♡	4◇
4NT	5◇	?	

There are various conventional ways in which North can indicate the number of aces he holds. For example, a scheme known as DOPI exhorts him to double with no ace, to pass with one ace, to bid the next suit (here 5♡) with two aces, and so on. This is playable, but there are times when the responder to 4NT is nervous of any advance to a slam and has a clear preference for defending; he may wish to signify this with a penalty double. When this scheme is played North has these possibilities:

Double	No liking for a slam
Pass	May have one ace but not enthusiastic
5♡	One ace
5♠	Two aces

10

Doubles and Redoubles

Take-out doubles are so familiar that one scarcely thinks of them as a convention. It is amusing to recall that in the early 1920s a Major Browning, writing his feature in the *Sketch*, categorised the new informatory double as a despicable manoeuvre.

When is a double for take-out?

Much more often than it used to be, it must be said. In the old days a double was for take-out when made at the one- or two-level, when partner had not made a bid, and when made at the first opportunity. All these stipulations have fallen by the wayside.

Firstly, a double up to Three Hearts, at least, is primarily for take-out when the opponents have found a trump fit. For example:

West	North	East	South
1♡	Pass	3♡	Dble

or

West	North	East	South
1◇	Pass	1♡	Pass
2♡	Pass	Pass	Dble

In both cases South's double is for take-out based on the expectation that since East–West have a good fit so will North–South.

There is also the well-known 'responsive double':

West	North	East	South
1◇	Dble	3◇	Dble

South holds:

(1)   ♠ J983   ♡ KJ76   ◇ J94   ♣ K7

South's double shows the values to compete but no particularly good suit to bid; it asks North to choose a suit. It would be unproductive to use such a double for penalties when the opponents have found a good fit.

The same principle applies in this slightly different auction:

West	North	East	South
1◇	1♠	2◇	Dble

South may have this hand:

(2)   ♠ 83   ♡ AK72   ◇ 103   ♣ KJ854

Again the opponents have found a fit, so South's double is not for penalties. It is known as a 'competitive double' and shows both the unbid suits, along with some tolerance for partner's suit, usually a doubleton.

This auction is similar:

West	North	East	South
1♣	1♠	2♣	2♡
3♣	Dble		

North holds such as:

(3)   ♠ AQJ86   ♡ Q2   ◇ KJ104   ♣ 62

He wants to compete in some direction and leaves the decision to his partner. With all-round values South may well decide to leave the double in.

What do you make of this slightly unusual auction?

West	North	East	South
1♢	1♠	2♢	2♠
3♢	Dble		

North–South have found a spade fit, so the double can hardly be for take-out. Neither would it be sensible to play it as an out-and-out penalty double. The best idea is to give it this meaning: 'pass the double if you have a defensive card or two, otherwise press on to 3♠'. North might hold:

(4)   ♠ AK1073   ♡ A94   ♢ 1063   ♣ K8

In effect the message is the same as before: I want to compete further but I am unsure which is the best direction.

Pressing hard in the part-score area is an extremely important part of the game. If you lose 50 when otherwise the opponents would have entered 60 below (at rubber bridge) you have in reality gained the hidden value of a part score – more than 100 points. And if you make the part score instead of them, the swing is almost equal to bidding and making a game. (See Chapter 13 – the Mathematics of the Auction.) The same sort of reasoning applies to duplicate; the difference between −110 and +110 is a full 6 IMPs.

What is the minimum for a take-out double?

Suppose your right-hand opponent opens 1♡. Would you double on this?

(5)   ♠ J1073   ♡ –   ♢ KQ62   ♣ KJ954

Some players would, we know, but on this shape a double is misguided. Partner may respond in no-trumps, which will play poorly. Or, after some competition, partner may double a part score in hearts, and in this case it will be a disadvantage that you cannot lead a trump. Basically, there is no need to enter the auction at this stage; if the opponents let the bidding drop at a low level, your side can take action then.

The same is true on this:

(6)   ♠ J976   ♡ 5   ◇ KQ53   ♣ KQ96

This is a point stronger but 4–4–4–1 is not such a good shape for a borderline double as players tend to think. The lack of a 5-card suit may be felt; also these types are strong in defence.

Suppose, next, that the opening in front of you is 1♠ and you hold this hand:

(7)   ♠ 7   ♡ KJ84   ◇ A10752   ♣ KJ3

Here you have a minimum, but acceptable, double. Since take-out doubles tend to draw partner's attention to any unbid major, a double would not be sound if the hearts and clubs on this hand were reversed.

Responding to a take-out double

As well as suggesting a possible denomination, your response to a take-out double must paint some picture of your general strength. Suppose the opponents open 1◇, your partner doubles, and the next player passes. You have a wealth of options open to you:

1♡/1♠/2♣	About 0–8 points
1NT	Diamond stop(s), about 6–9 points
2♡/2♠/3♣	About 8–10 points, non-forcing
2◇	11+ points, forcing to 'suit agreement' (see below)
2NT	Diamond stop(s), about 10–12 points
3♡/3♠	Long suit but only around 7–9 points
Game bids	To play

So much for the theory. Let's see some actual hands, again assuming that partner has made a take-out double of 1♢.

    (8)   ♠ 103   ♡ J872   ♢ 973   ♣ AQJ4

Here you would respond 1♡, preferring to show the major even though the clubs are stronger. You are not quite worth a jump response to 2♡.

    (9)   ♠ A10954   ♡ 52   ♢ 874   ♣ KJ4

This is about dead centre for a jump response, here 2♠. With no special fit for spades, and a double in the lower range, partner will then pass.

    (10)   ♠ 6   ♡ AQ10752   ♢ 932   ♣ K106

Here you are worth 4♡. If you doubt it, write down some minimum hands for partner's double. You will probably find that game is cold.

The auction following a cue-bid response

When the responder to the double has a hand of 11 points or more, he can start by showing his strength with a cue bid. The bidding must then continue until the partnership has found a fit.

West	East	West	North	East	South
♠AJ87	♠KQ53	–	–	–	1♣
♡K102	♡A973	Dble	Pass	2♣	Pass
♢KQJ65	♢93	2♢	Pass	2♡	Pass
♣8	♣Q105	2♠	Pass	3♠	Pass
		4♠	End		

East shows his strength with a cue bid and the partnership then makes a series of (forcing) suit bids. East's 3♠ call is non-forcing because a suit has been agreed, but West has enough to advance to game.

Second-round action by the doubler

A single raise of responder's major-suit response does not promise
the earth. On an auction like this:

West	North	East	South
1◇	Dble	Pass	1♠
Pass	2♠		

You might, as North, hold this type of hand:

(11)   ♠ AQ92   ♡ KQ83   ◇ 96   ♣ AJ4

You are not so much inviting game as confirming that there is a fit
and preventing East from backing into the auction at a cheap level.
   On nearly all minimum doubles you will pass your partner's
simple suit response. When instead you follow your double by
introducing a new suit you show extra values. This would be a typical
auction:

West	East	West	North	East	South
♠A4	♠K1076	–	–	–	1◇
♡AQJ65	♡K72	Dble	Pass	1♠	Pass
◇K2	◇105	2♡	Pass	4♡	End
♣K1082	♣J953				

Over a jump response, suggesting about 8–10 points (a sequence
such as 1♣-Dble-Pass-2♡), a subsequent change of suit by the
doubler is forcing.

Leaving in a take-out double for penalties

When your trumps lie over the potential declarer, leaving in partner's take-out double is often an attractive option. Suppose, at love
all, the bidding starts like this:

West	North	East	South
–	–	–	1♡
Pass	Pass	Dble	Pass
?			

and, as West, you hold:

(12)   ♠ 93   ♡ KJ52   ◇ J105   ♣ AQ74

If you pass out the double you can expect to make two hearts, two clubs, possibly a spade ruff too. This is in addition to whatever tricks partner may produce. There is every chance of a useful 300 or 500, with game your way an uncertain proposition.

Suppose that you held the same hand after this auction:

West	North	East	South
–	1♡	Dble	Pass
?			

With your trumps sitting *under* declarer it would be an unattractive gamble to pass out the double. You should bid 2NT instead. On the sequence shown above you should leave in a double only when your trumps are robust enough to stand a trump lead. That's because you will need to draw declarer's trumps to obtain any sort of penalty.

(13)   ♠ 5   ♡ KQJ92   ◇ 10874   ♣ K93

Here you could leave in a double of 1♡, expecting partner to lead a trump.

Action by third hand after a take-out double

After a start such as 1♠ – Dble – ? you should raise partner's suit on the slightest support.

(14)   ♠ Q1084   ♡ 10762   ◇ J53   ♣ 84

You have a good fit; the opponents will doubtless have a good fit too. Make life awkward for them by raising to 2♠.

(15)   ♠ K1072   ♡ 7   ◇ Q9643   ♣ J108

Here, without a double, you would raise to 2♠. Over a double you make it 3♠.

(16)   ♠ QJ72   ♡ K4   ◇ A1093   ♣ J32

With a hand worth a normal double raise you bid a conventional 2NT over the double. This is a standard manoeuvre, even at rubber bridge.

Let's turn now to hands where you do not have a fit for partner. In this area there have been two recent changes of style, both sensible.

West	North	East	South
1◇	Dble	1♠	

A change of suit over a double used to be treated as non-forcing, possibly a rescue. The modern idea is that it is better to develop your own auction in a natural way; East's 1♠ call is therefore forcing. This style is known as 'ignoring the double'. A consequence is that if East instead bids 2♠ over the double, this becomes pre-emptive, on such as KJ108xx and not much else.

Since good responding hands can be launched with a simple change of suit over the double, the redouble is mainly restricted to those occasions where you see fair prospect of a penalty.

(17)   ♠ 7   ♡ K1063   ◇ AJ6   ♣ J9432

When partner opens 1♠ and the next player doubles, you redouble. Knowing that you are out for the kill, partner may be able to double the next player's call when holding only three trumps. A defensive combination of 3–3 in the trump suit often works well.

Action by fourth player over a redouble

Suppose you are fourth to speak and the bidding starts like this:

West	North	East	South
1♡	Dble	Rdble	?

You are under attack: the opponents are hoping to double you somewhere. It is vital that you do not bypass your safest hiding place. You may hold:

(18)   ♠ 762   ♡ 1062   ◇ Q54   ♣ J954

Without the redouble you would have had to respond 2♣. Now, though, you don't have to speak. You should pass, giving partner the chance to seek refuge in 1♠. An immediate bid of 2♣ from you would imply a 5-card suit.

You should step warily even when you do hold a 5-card suit.

(19)   ♠ 1053   ♡ 982   ◇ J9542   ♣ 76

After the same start of 1♡ – Dble – Rdble, you should again pass, hoping that partner will bid a black suit and not be doubled there. If the axe does fall you can consider a removal to 2◇.

Stronger bids by the fourth player, such as a jump bid or a cue bid, hold their meanings after a redouble. You must have some way to show a good hand.

When to make a penalty double

Be wary of doubling freely bid games just because you hold a lot of points. Suppose the bidding goes like this:

West	North	East	South
–	–	–	1♠
1NT	2♠	Pass	4♠
?			

As West, you hold:

(20)   ♠ A92   ♡ AK104   ◇ KJ3   ♣ K87

Many players would double now, but there's no logic behind it. Nobody forced South to bid 4♠; he obviously has a very distributional hand, perhaps a two-suiter with a singleton or void heart. Above all, you don't *need* to double; if South has overbid and goes one down you will score well anyway.

The key point on hands like this is that you hold no unpleasant surprise for declarer. He knew that he was missing all those aces and kings when he decided to bid 4♠. The time to double is when you hold tricks, usually trump tricks, that declarer is not expecting to lose.

The auction may go this way:

West	North	East	South
–	–	–	1♠
Pass	2♣	Pass	2♠
Pass	3♠	Pass	4♠
?			

Your hand, as West, is:

(21)   ♠ QJ92   ♡ 1082   ◇ KQJ42   ♣ 5

Only 9 points, but this represents a much more promising double than the previous hand. Declarer was certainly not expecting to lose two trump tricks when he ventured 4♠; also, your singleton club suggests that dummy's main side suit may be breaking poorly. Another important consideration is that the opponents' auction was limited, indicating that they have no values to spare.

Surprising as it may seem, most of the biggest penalties come from low-level contracts. That's because a player's first call in the auction is usually a step into the dark; if his partner has nothing, he may find himself well short of the required number of tricks.

Suppose the bidding starts like this:

West	North	East	South
1♠	2◇	?	

and, as East, you are looking at:

(22)   ♠ 7   ♡ AQ42   ◇ A105   ♣ 109862

A penalty double is your best chance of a worthwhile score. On a good day you might find partner with a singleton heart or club and pick up 800 or so in the cross-fire.

The Business Redouble

To make a contract such as 4♡ doubled rarely gives you a bad board. For that reason you should be wary of making a greedy redouble when there is any chance that the opponents may take flight into a relatively cheap spot their way.

South could not resist the temptation on this deal from a team-of-four match:

North–South game, dealer South

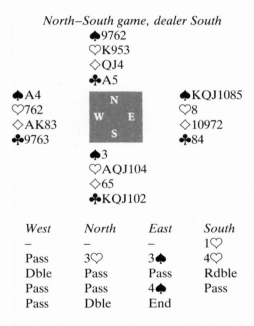

```
                    ♠9762
                    ♡K953
                    ◇QJ4
                    ♣A5
    ♠A4                              ♠KQJ1085
    ♡762                             ♡8
    ◇AK83                            ◇10972
    ♣9763                            ♣84
                    ♠3
                    ♡AQJ104
                    ◇65
                    ♣KQJ102
```

West	North	East	South
–	–	–	1♡
Pass	3♡	3♠	4♡
Dble	Pass	Pass	Rdble
Pass	Pass	4♠	Pass
Pass	Dble	End	

South felt it a near certainty that North would cover two of his five losers and expressed this opinion with a redouble. This was too much for East who retreated to four spades. The result was that North–South collected a miserly 100 instead of the 790 that was previously heading in their direction.

The time to redouble is when you think your own contract will be touch-and-go, one down at most, but you will be happy to deal with any enemy retreat.

11

When to Overcall

There is a 1♣ opening to your right and you overcall 1♠ on a hand such as:

(1) ♠ KQJ92 ♡ 853 ♢ A5 ♣ 764

What have you achieved by such a bid? All these good things:

(a) You may win the auction, playing in spades at some level;
(b) you have robbed the opponents of bidding space – the third player cannot respond 1♢ or 1♡ and his hand may now be unsuitable for 1NT;
(c) you have suggested a good opening lead to partner.

Nor have you had to risk anything much in the process; the playing strength offered by your good spade suit will protect you from a big penalty. In short, 1♠ on such a hand is a near-perfect overcall.

Now suppose there is a 1♢ opening to your right and you hold:

(2) ♠ A2 ♡ Q8654 ♢ 976 ♣ K54

There are players by the thousand who will overcall 1♡ on this, seeing no difference. What is the point of it? Your shortage in spades means that you are unlikely to win the auction; you're not taking any bidding space from the opponents, nor are you bidding a suit that cries out to be led. In short, it is poor tactics to overcall on such hands. You are simply giving helpful information to the opponents.

When a one-level overcall will consume space or suggest a good lead, a 4-card suit will do. Suppose right-hand opponent opens 1♢ and you hold:

(3)   ♠ KQ105   ♡ 862   ◇ A1042   ♣ Q3

Although the suit is poor, it is reasonable to venture a 1♠ overcall. It prevents the third player responding 1♡ and may frighten the opponents from a makable no-trump contract.

When you make a two-level overcall the risk of being doubled is greater. To require a fair suit for such a bid is therefore not a question of nervousness but one of commonsense. There is a 1♡ opening on your right and you hold:

(4)   ♠ A103   ♡ Q85   ◇ J3   ♣ AQ863

Even though you hold the values for an opening bid your hand is not at all suitable for a 2♣ overcall, whatever the vulnerability. It's the type of hand where you could go three down doubled and find that the opponents could not make a game. The clubs are simply not good enough. Suppose instead you hold this hand:

(5)   ♠ 982   ♡ 4   ◇ A103   ♣ KQ10872

Now you don't have the general values to open the bidding but, non-vulnerable, you are worth a 2♣ overcall. You have fair playing strength and would like a club lead.

Overcall or double?

Some hands offer a choice between a take-out double and an overcall. What would you bid over 1♡, holding these cards:

(6)   ♠ KQ54   ♡ A5   ◇ J4   ♣ A10952

An overcall of 2♣ would hardly describe your hand; for one thing, only 4 of your 14 points are in clubs. Nor would it necessarily leave you in the right spot. It is better to double. If partner responds 2◇, the most expensive suit, he is likely to hold five cards there.

The situation is different when the five-card suit is a major:

(7)   ♠ KJ1054   ♡ 5   ◇ K102   ♣ AQ73

Now, even though your shape is very suitable for a take-out double of 1♡, it is preferable to start with 1♠; otherwise the spade suit might not gain a mention. If the bidding continues in this vein:

West	North	East	South
1♡	1♠	2♡	Pass
Pass	?		

you can compete with a take-out double on the second round, inviting partner to pick the best spot.

Responding to overcalls

When your partner overcalls at the one level, not vulnerable, his normal range will be between 8 and 14 points. Initially you should credit him with something close to the lower level.

West	North	East	South
1◇	1♠	Pass	?

Here 1NT by South would suggest about 10–12 points, 2NT 13–14. In this area, of course, points are not everything. The nature of the guard in the opener's suit is critical; you would rather hold Q10xx than Axx.

How would you assess South's intentions in a sequence like this:

West	North	East	South
1◇	1♡	Pass	2♣

There are two ways of interpreting South's 2♣. Do you think of it as a 'denial' bid, meaning 'I don't like hearts very much, clubs might be better', or as constructive, implying 'Maybe we can go somewhere'? Nowadays most players favour this second interpretation. This makes good sense since with a poor hand you won't go far wrong by passing 1♡.

When you have support for partner's overcall you must express it in one way or another. Suppose, after a start of 1◇ – 1♠ – Pass – ?, you have this hand:

(8)   ♠ K104   ♡ 105   ◇ 9643   ♣ KJ82

Raise to 2♠. Such a call cramps the opener, who doubtless has a fair hand.

Now give yourself a shade more:

(9)   ♠ AJ53   ♡ Q10752   ◇ J84   ♣ 6

On this hand you would raise to 3♠. Any direct raises in spades will be understood to have an element of pre-emption about them. Clearly you must find some other type of response when you are stronger, with serious game prospects:

(10)   ♠ A106   ♡ K972   ◇ 75   ♣ AQ84

With this type of hand, a constructive raise based on high-card points is expressed by a cue bid in the enemy suit, here 2◇. Partner will rebid just 2♠ with a moderate overcall, make some more encouraging noise otherwise. If partner does rebid simply 2♠ it would be close, on this hand, whether you should make any further advance. Vulnerable, you might give him 3♠; non-vulnerable, you might pass.

Jump overcalls

There are basically two popular styles of jump overcall (such as 2♡ over an opening 1◇): weak and intermediate. The weak style is used by many in the tournament world, particularly in the US; the intermediate style is popular elsewhere and is fairly standard at rubber bridge.

We will look at weak jump overcalls first. They vary somewhat according to vulnerability, but suggest about 6–10 points. Over one of a minor, non-vulnerable, followers of this style would venture 2♠ on:

(11)   ♠ K109864   ♡ 743   ◇ J   ♣ Q85

Vulnerable, something nearer the top of the range would be preferable:

(12)   ♠ KQ10753   ♡ 5   ◇ Q6   ♣ Q952

These weak jump overcalls presumably cause embarrassment on occasions, but they also give away a good deal of information which may later be helpful to the opponents. They have another, indirect, disadvantage: a fair number of hands become difficult to express. For example, an opponent opens 1◇ and you hold:

(13)   ♠ 7   ♡ AQJ842   ◇ K65   ♣ A32

If 2♡ would be a weak call you have to choose between 1♡ and double. A simple 1♡ could easily lead to a missed game. If instead you double, your partner may leap in spades and be unimpressed by your spade support. Even if partner responds only 1♠ to your double, it will not be clear, when you continue with 2♡, whether you have a single-suiter or perhaps 2–5–2–4 distribution.

We much prefer the intermediate jump overcall. The accepted standard is a 6-card suit and opening values, the sort of hand on which you would open the long suit and rebid it over a 1NT response.

(14)   ♠ AQ9842   ♡ K86   ◇ A10   ♣ 43

This is a typical 2♠ overcall. Vulnerability makes a difference, naturally; when not vulnerable, particularly when partner has passed, you may lower the standard a bit.

An advantage of this style is that the playing values of a simple overcall are more restricted and so easier to judge. When a partner who had available an intermediate 2♠ overcall chooses to bid only 1♠, there is no need for you to keep the bidding alive 'in case you had a good hand, partner'.

There are no special problems when responding to an intermediate jump overcall. Obviously there is no need to 'rescue' partner from such a call, so a change of suit by responder should be treated as forcing. When you have a fit for partner's jump overcall in a major suit, the same principles apply as with a simple overcall. A direct raise may have an element of pre-emption to it; when you hold a sound raise you should cue-bid instead.

> (15)   ♠ K102   ♡ A873   ◇ 10654   ♣ J7

After 1◇ on your left, 2♠ intermediate from partner, and a pass on your right, you should cue-bid 3◇. This shows a high-card raise to 3♠ and invites partner to bid the game.

A direct raise to 3♠ would show something more like this:

> (16)   ♠ Q972   ♡ 7   ◇ 1093   ♣ K7642

There is still a distant chance of game and partner may advance if he wishes.

12

Protection

When the opponents stop bidding at a low level it is reasonable to assume that the points are fairly evenly divided between the two sides. It is important not to sell out too cheaply in this situation and the major responsibility for competing lies with the player in the pass-out seat.

Suppose the bidding starts in this modest fashion:

West	North	East	South
1♡	Pass	Pass	?

and, sitting South, you hold these cards:

(1) ♠ A1094   ♡ 5   ♢ Q10863   ♣ K75

It is losing bridge to pass now. You can tell from the opponents' lack of ambition that your partner holds fair values. His lips are sealed for the moment, so you must move on your side's behalf; you should compete with a take-out double. Nine points is perhaps below the normal standard, but this is a particularly strong nine points, with good preparedness and strong intermediates.

In general it is right to compete in the pass-out position, either with a double or an overcall, on roughly a king less than you would need when sitting directly over the opener. Of course your partner must bear this in mind when considering his response. Here is a complete deal involving fourth-seat protection:

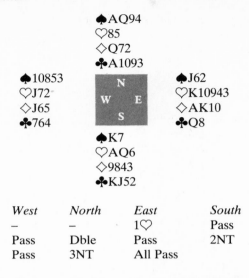

	♠AQ94	
	♡85	
	◇Q72	
	♣A1093	

	♠AQ94	
♠10853		♠J62
♡J72		♡K10943
◇J65		◇AK10
♣764		♣Q8
	♠K7	
	♡AQ6	
	◇9843	
	♣KJ52	

West	North	East	South
–	–	1♡	Pass
Pass	Dble	Pass	2NT
Pass	3NT	All Pass	

When North competes with a take-out double South must decide how many no-trumps to bid. His hand would justify a 3NT response, facing a second-hand double. Allowing for the fact that North's double was in the protective seat, he responds only 2NT. The spotlight switches back to North, who advances to game, reckoning that his initial double could have been made on a point or two less.

The protective 1NT

A 1NT overcall in the second seat shows good values, around 15–17 points. In the fourth seat, though, after a start such as 1♡ – Pass – Pass, it makes sense to lower the requirements. A protective 1NT overcall shows around 11–14 points, this type of hand:

   (2)   ♠ K4   ♡ A105   ◇ Q962   ♣ A854

A double of 1♡ is unattractive with only two cards in the unbid major. If 1NT were not available you would be stuck for a bid.

A protective 1NT is often the best answer even when you don't have a secure guard in the opener's suit:

    (3)   ♠ A52   ♡ 1094   ♢ AK103   ♣ Q87

When 1♡ runs to you a call of 1NT shows the type and is more likely to lead to a sensible spot than a double. If 1NT is passed out and the opener reels off five hearts, this will not be a disaster.

Protective overcalls

Simple overcalls in the pass-out position may be made on quite weak hands with a moderate suit.

    (4)   ♠ 632   ♡ AQ952   ♢ 85   ♣ Q104

If 1♢ ran to you, you would protect with 1♡.

The standards for an intermediate jump overcall are similarly lowered in the fourth seat. Any hand with a 6-card suit and close to opening values will qualify. After 1♢ has been followed by two passes you hold:

    (5)   ♠ Q4   ♡ KQJ752   ♢ 65   ♣ K82

You are worth 2♡. Let's make the hand a bit stronger:

    (6)   ♠ A4   ♡ KQ10753   ♢ 82   ♣ KQ7

Now you are too strong for 2♡ in the protective seat. Start with a double and bid hearts on the next round.

A cue bid in the fourth seat need not be a giant. It is the best move when you have a strong two-suiter and no other convenient way to launch a counter-attack. Suppose 1♡ is passed round and you hold:

(7)   ♠ AQ872   ♡ –   ◇ KJ9743   ♣ K5

If you start with a double and partner decides to pass for penalties you will feel decidedly uncomfortable. A better idea is 2♡. This is not forcing for ever! It simply gives you a chance to find the best fit. For example, if partner responded 2♠ you would raise to 3♠, non-forcing.

Protection when opponents find a fit

What conclusions do you draw when an auction starts like this:

West	North	East	South
1♡	Pass	2♡	Pass
Pass	?		

The opponents have made no move towards game, even though they have found a major-suit fit. You can bet your last dollar that the points are evenly divided between the two sides.

Another important consideration is this – when the opponents have found a fit, *you will have a fit somewhere too*. Why is that? Suppose the opponents have 9 hearts between them. You and your partner will hold only 4 hearts between you. With 22 cards in the other three suits you are guaranteed a fit of at least 8 cards somewhere.

Take these two factors together – you have half the points and a very likely fit somewhere – and it becomes clear that the odds strongly favour competing for the part score.

After the auction we noted, the opponents stopping in 2♡, you might hold this hand:

(8)   ♠ KJ76   ♡ 82   ◇ A103   ♣ Q954

Not enough to set the world on fire but you should double. Nearly always partner will have at least 8 points and you will have a playable spot somewhere. There are three ways in which the double may gain: you may make your contract; go one down when they could have made their contract; or you may push them up a level.

Suppose your hand is not suitable for a double:

(9) ♠ AJ92 ♡ J762 ♢ A1093 ♣ 8

Still, the odds are good that you have a fit somewhere. Reopen with 2♠ on the 4-card suit. On the odd occasions when partner has a 2–1–5–5 shape, it may occur to him that you were unable to overcall 1♠ on the first round and may have only a 4-card spade suit. He will advance to 3♣ and you can then move to 3♢.

(10) ♠ 102 ♡ Q5 ♢ KJ93 ♣ A10872

Here you would compete with 2NT, the Unusual No-trump showing the minor suits (*see* Chapter 14). You may think that such a call is dangerous. There is an element of danger, it is true, but much more damage is done in the long run if you fail to make such calls. The opponents will then win the argument on too many part-score deals.

When not to protect

Sometimes the opponents stop low but there are warning signs that protection may be unwise. Perhaps the bidding starts

West	*North*	*East*	*South*
1♣	Pass	Pass	?

and, as South, you hold:

(11) ♠ 52 ♡ K10642 ♢ J9 ♣ AQ102

You have enough to bid 1♡ but since partner passed over 1♣ he can hardly hold much of value. Also, who holds the spades? Maybe East–West have a spade fit, which will come to light if you permit another round of bidding. It is wisest to pass.

We mentioned that conditions for protection are at their most favourable when the opponents have found a fit. The opposite is the case when the bidding goes something like this:

West	North	East	South
1◇	Pass	1♠	Pass
2♣	Pass	Pass	?

South holds:

(12)　　　♠ A43　　　♡ KQ1085　　　◇ Q63　　　♣ 107

Here it is quite possible for the opener to hold 16 points or so and East a misfitting 8 or 9. If you enter with 2♡ you may well find yourself shelling out 500, with nothing on for the opposition.

13

The Mathematics of the Auction

In this section we consider some of the mathematical truths of the auction, especially at rubber bridge. We look first at the relative values of part score, game and slam; then at the expectations relating to sacrifices and penalty doubles. If figures bother you, just study the conclusions, which *are* important.

Contesting the part score

How high would you put the value of a part score of 40 or 60? In tournament play a bonus of 50 is added, so that two hearts just made gives you 110. This bonus of 50 is a considerable underestimate of the value of a part score at rubber bridge, though. A closer evaluation would be about 120 in the early stages and something over 150 at Game All. So, at rubber bridge, it is a fair exchange to go down 200 to save a part score of 40 or 60. This does not apply when you are partnered by the village idiot, of course; then it would be foolish to prolong the rubber.

Part score or game?

What odds do you need to try for game at *IMP scoring*? It's fairly easy to work it out. Suppose you're non-vulnerable. If the game is on and the opponents don't bid it, you will score 420 against 170, a gain of 6 IMPs. If the game goes one down you will score −50 against 140, a loss of 5 IMPs. So, you should attempt games that are slightly odds against.

When you are vulnerable you will gain 10 IMPs when the game makes and lose 6 IMPs when it fails, so you can afford to bid games that are appreciably less than a 50% shot.

At *rubber bridge*, as we mentioned above, a part score is more valuable; you are consequently less inclined to risk surrendering it by failing in a borderline game. The hidden value of the first or second game is about 350, of the third game 500. So, bidding a close game at love all will net you an extra 230 (the hidden value of game, 350, minus the hidden value of the part score, 120) when it makes. When the game goes one down, this will cost you 260 (90 for the lost trick value, 120 for the hidden value of the part score, 50 for the actual penalty). Conclusion: you should not bid games unless they are somewhat odds on.

The position is similar at game all. Bidding a close game will gain you 350 (500 − 150) when it makes, cost you 340 (90 + 150 + 100) when it goes one down. So, a game needs to be a 50% proposition to be worth bidding. This contrasts sharply with the odds at IMP play.

When should you bid a close game at *duplicate pairs*? In theory whenever the game is better than a 50% shot. It is worth remembering, though, that when a game contract superficially depends on a 50–50 finesse there are generally other small hazards – a bad break in the main suit or an unexpected ruff.

The conclusion is that at rubber bridge or at pairs play it is wrong to strain for game. If you can settle in two of a major, even two of a minor, and are doubtful about game prospects, take the plus score.

Game or slam?

What odds do you need to bid a small slam at love all? Again it is easy to calculate. If the slam succeeds you will gain an extra 500 points. If it goes one down you will lose the value of the game (300 at duplicate, about 350 at rubber bridge) plus the tricks (100 odd) plus the penalty (50). This, too, comes to around 500 and many books will therefore tell you that it is fair to bid a small slam on an even chance.

This is true in mathematical terms, but there is another consideration when you are wondering whether to advance from, say, a base of 4♡ or 4♠. If your slam try is met by an unenthusiastic response and you finally subside at the five level, there are times when even that will fail. Also, in a duplicate match, there will sometimes be an 'oddity' at the other table, so that just bidding game will result in a good swing.

It comes to this: be cautious about trying for a slam; don't go beyond game if a bad break might defeat you at the five level.

Small slam or grand slam?

To proceed from a small slam to be a grand slam at *rubber bridge* you need, in mathematical terms, odds of over 2 to 1 in your favour. These things can never be calculated exactly, so in practice avoid grand slams unless you can just about count the tricks.

The odds of 2 to 1 apply to *IMP scoring* too, but only when you can be certain that the pair holding your cards in the other room are certain to be in at least the small slam. Nothing is more annoying than to go one down, unluckily, in a grand slam and find that your opponents did not venture past game.

At *pairs* it is right to bid a grand slam that is slightly odds-on, but again this applies only when the whole field will be in six at least. In practice you will nearly always find a few pairs missing the simplest of slams. Also, you can often score well at the six level by contracting for a slightly hazardous 6NT. In short, bid an uncertain grand slam only when you know you need the points.

Sacrifice bidding

Good judgment in sacrifice situations is one of the hardest areas of the game. The first point to make is that whereas it may be worthwhile to concede 500 against an enemy 620 at pairs play, this is not worth very much at IMPs, still less at rubber bridge.

Suppose they bid a thin vulnerable 4♡ against you at *IMP scoring*. If you sacrifice in 4♠ and lose 500, you will gain 3 IMPs only if your other pair have bid and made the heart game. If they have +170 on their card, conceding 500 will cost you a bundle; it's better to hope that the heart game fails. It's the same in *pairs*. A finely judged −500 against what would have been 620 the other way is not much use unless a fair number of pairs have bid the game.

Against this, there is always the chance that when you sacrifice the opponents may misjudge the situation and bid one more their way instead of doubling you. All one can say is that there is a lot more to it than mathematics!

Penalty doubles

Penalty doubles are not well rewarded on the scoresheet. Suppose, for example, that you decide to double non-vulnerable opponents in four hearts. If they make it they score an extra 120 below, plus 50 for the insult, a total of 170. If you get them one down you increase the penalty by a measly 50. In other words, when the decision is fairly close you are laying 7 to 2 on your double being right.

Two other factors weigh against penalty doubles of freely bid contracts. The mere fact that you have doubled is quite likely to tell against you in the play; nothing is more costly than a double that leads declarer to the winning line. Also, opponents who have an unexpected void, cutting off one or more of your expected tricks in defence, may decide to redouble. So, except at pairs, it is rarely right to double a freely bid contract unless you expect it to go two down.

Close doubles of part scores are not part of the rubber or IMP game, but are sometimes a necessary risk in a pairs. When opponents are vulnerable one down doubled will give you 200, a valuable prize. In that situation a successful close double can translate your score from 30% to 90% (when others have made a partial your way or accepted a penalty of 100).

14

Bidding Conventions

Bidding conventions come and (fortunately) go. In this section we mention, in alphabetical order, the best of the conventions that are currently popular. If you are playing with an unfamiliar partner you will, of course, need to check his preferences. Meanwhile, it is useful to know what your opponents are up to.

ASPRO DEFENCE TO 1NT

A variant of the Astro defence (see below) where an overcall of 2♣ shows hearts and another suit, an overcall of 2◇ shows spades and a minor.

ASTRO DEFENCE TO 1NT

There is limited value in natural overcalls of 2♣ and 2◇ over an opponent's 1NT since you will often be outbid in a major. Most defensive systems over 1NT therefore assign an artificial meaning to such minor-suit overcalls.

South	*West*	*North*	*East*
1NT	2♣ or 2◇		

South	*West*	*North*	*East*
1NT	Pass	Pass	2♣ or 2◇

In each of these sequences an Astro 2♣ overcall shows hearts and a minor suit, 2◇ shows spades and any second suit. There should be at least nine cards in the two suits. These are typical Astro hands:

	(1)	(2)		(3)	
	♠KJ95		♠6		♠A8642
	♡K4		♡Q10863		♡K5
	◇AQ862		◇KJ1076		◇3
	♣95		♣K2		♣KQ732

The Astrologist would overcall 2◇ on (1) and (3), 2♣ on (2).
The responder to an Astro bid has several options:

(a)   Limit bid in partner's known major
(b)   Pass of the Astro bid with length there and nowhere else
(c)   2NT, a limit bid
(d)   Occasionally a new suit of at least 6 cards, non-forcing
(e)   A raise of the artificial suit, the only force
(f)   When in doubt, the intermediate suit, 2◇ over 2♣, 2♡ over 2◇. These bids are not forcing.

Here is a typical Astro sequence, East–West jockeying for a fit:

West	East	South	West	North	East
♠AQ108	♠64	1NT	2◇	No	2♡
♡42	♡K1087	No	3♣	End	
◇Q7	◇K964				
♣AQ972	♣1085				

West shows spades and another suit. East, with only two cards in the indicated major, responds in the intermediate suit, happy to play there should hearts be his partner's second suit. West would rebid 2♠ with a 5-card suit, which East would pass. His actual 3♣ rebid indicates four spades and five or six clubs.

Assessment.   This is a good method when you hold a two-suiter, either 5–5 or 5–4. With only four cards in the indicated major you need a better than minimum hand and a stocky major suit, such as KQJx.

BARON 2NT RESPONSE

A Baron 2NT response to one of a suit is forcing and shows a
balanced hand of at least 16 points. Both players may then make
natural bids on the way to 3NT.

West	*East*	*West*	*East*
♠AJ87	♠KQ53	1♡	2NT
♡KQ863	♡J2	3♡	3♠
◇Q3	◇A106	4♠	End
♣105	♣KQJ4		

Here West shows his fifth heart rather than bidding spades at his
second turn. He knows that his partner can introduce spades if there
is a fit there. (The sequence 1♡ – 2NT – 3♠ would in fact show that
the opener was 4–4 in the majors, since West would rebid his hearts
on a 5-card suit). Note that East has already issued a mild slam
invitation with his 2NT call. When partner can bid only 4♠ over 3♠,
rather than cue-bid in a minor, East has no reason to consider a
further move.

Playing this style, you cannot use the 2NT response on flat hands
of 11–12 points. You have to respond in a suit, intending to bid 2NT
on the second round.

Assessment. The principal value of the style is that it provides good
cover for those balanced 16–18 point hands that are sometimes
difficult to express. In tournament play the method has gained
widespread acceptance. Against that, most rubber bridge players
are reluctant to abandon the natural 11–12 point 2NT response.

BENJAMIN TWO BIDS

This is a way of combining strong and weak openings at the two level.

2♣	shows a hand of Acol two strength in any of the four suits. The negative response is 2◇ and a minimum rebid by the opener (a sequence such as 2♣ – 2◇ – 3♣) may be passed
2◇	shows a standard Acol 2♣ bid, with all sequences forcing to game. The negative response is now 2♡
2♡/2♠	weak, in principle a 6-card suit and 6–10 points

Both 2♣ and 2◇ are available for strong no-trump types. The recommended scheme is:

2NT	20–22 points
2♣ – 2◇ – 2NT	23–24 points
2◇ – 2♡ – 2NT	25–26 points
2♣ – 2◇ – 3NT	27–28 points
2◇ – 2♡ – 3NT	29–30 points

This is especially advantageous on the 25–26 point hands where a 3NT rebid was previously necessary. Now there is room for a Baron 3♣ or some other response at the three level.

Assessment. This method must be reckoned an improvement on the old Acol style, because it expresses both strong and weak types at the two level.

COMPETITIVE DOUBLES

When the opponents find a fit it rarely makes sense to double for penalties at a low level. It follows that doubles in auctions such as the following are best played as *competitive*, for take-out.

	South	West	North	East
(a)	1♠	2♣	2♡	3♣
	Dble			
(b)	1♠	2♢	2♠	Dble

The meaning of the double in both cases is 'I have the values to compete but no good bid to make.'

Many players extend the idea to auctions of this type:

South	West	North	East
1♡	1♠	2♢	Dble

Since North's 2♢ is generally played as forcing, there would be little point in a penalty double. East's double is competitive, showing in this case a club suit and tolerance (usually doubleton support) for spades.

Assessment.   Battling for the part score is an important area of the game, particularly when the opponents have found a fit. The competitive double is an invaluable weapon in this situation and is very common in tournament play.

CROWHURST TWO CLUBS

A sequence such as 1♢ – 1♡ – 1NT normally shows 12–14 when you are playing a strong no-trump, 15–16 when you are playing a weak no-trump. Playing the Crowhurst convention, opener may rebid 1NT on a wider range, 12–16, whatever no-trump is being used. To obtain further definition of the opener's hand, responder may bid a Crowhurst 2♣ (conventional even if the opening bid was 1♣). After a start of 1♢ – 1♡ – 1NT – 2♣ the opener rebids as follows:

2♢	Lower range, without three hearts or four spades
2♡	Lower range, 3-card heart support
2♠	Lower range, 4 spades
2NT	Upper range, 15–16 points (forcing to game)
3♡	Upper range, 3-card heart support

Assessment. An advantage of this scheme is that the opening bidder can develop his hand more naturally on hands where the 1NT rebid (not playing Crowhurst) would be inaccurate. For example, suppose you are playing a weak no-trump and hold:

    ♠ 75   ♡ AK73   ♢ J4   ♣ A10752

Playing Crowhurst, you can open 1♣ and rebid 1NT over 1♠.

A disadvantage of the wide-range rebid is that a responder with 10 points feels he has to advance in case his partner is maximum. This can lead to an uncomfortably high contract when the opener is minimum.

DEFENCE TO STRONG 1♣ OPENING

Many systems are based on a strong 1♣ opening, made on nearly all hands of 16–17 points or more. Since the opener has not yet named his best suit, it is tempting for the opponents to enter the auction, even on a weak hand, hoping to consume some space before it is the opener's turn to bid again.

There are various conventional schemes, some of which enable you to enter on almost any hand that contains two suits of 4 cards or longer. (For example, 1♡ might show two suits of the same colour, 1♠ two suits of the same rank.) When you are playing against good opposition it is foolish to use such methods. They will know how to counter your low-level intervention, sometimes even turning it to their advantage. Also, when they win the auction (as they nearly always will) they will play the hand much better, benefiting from the information gained in the auction.

So, the best idea is to play a relatively simple scheme, entering only when you have one or more suits with some substance:

Simple overcalls	natural
1NT	both majors
Jump overcalls	weak but natural
2NT	both minors

Assessment. When an opponent opens a strong 1♣, don't enter the auction thinking you can unbalance the opposition. You give the opponents a free warning that the suits are not breaking well and helpful information for when they play the hand.

DRURY

Partner opens 1♡ or 1♠ in third or fourth position and perhaps your natural response would be a double raise or 2NT. However, if he has opened light this may be too high. Drury is a way to escape the dilemma. As responder, you bid an artificial 2♣; the opener, if lower range, bids 2♢, which you may transfer to Two of the opener's major. (You mustn't pass 2♢.)

When the opener is well up to strength he may make some different rebid; or he may rebid 2♢ and advance later.

Assessment. Drury was popular for a time but has rather fallen out of sight (partly, in England at any rate, because the governing body ruled that it was an unfair method of fielding psyches!). It certainly has value in a pairs event, where third hand may hold such as ♠AQ10xx ♡xx ♢Kxxx ♣xx. It is reasonably safe, playing Drury, to open 1♠, not expecting to be carried beyond 2♠.

FIVE-ACE BLACKWOOD

In this version of Blackwood the king of the agreed trump suit is counted as an ace. These are the responses:

5♣	0 or 4 'aces'
5♦	1 or 5 'aces'
5♡	2 'aces'
5♠	3 'aces'

Assessment.   This is an improvement on standard Blackwood but less sophisticated than Roman Key Card Blackwood (*see* later).

FIVE-CARD MAJORS

In many parts of the world there is a general tendency towards guaranteeing at least a 5-card suit when you open 1♡ or 1♠. This method is often played in conjunction with a forcing 1NT response.

Assessment.   5-card majors in conjunction with short minor openings is certainly an easy method to play. Against that, the 4-card major openings favoured in systems such as Acol have pre-emptive value.

FIVE-CARD STAYMAN

It is fairly common to open 2NT (or follow a sequence such as 2♣ – 2♦ – 2NT) when you hold a 5-card major. Five-card Stayman is a convention that lets the responder detect 5–3 fits in a major, as well as 4–4 fits.

The responder bids 3♣ and the opener rebids along these lines:

3♦	No 5-card major
3♡	5 hearts
3♠	5 spades
3NT	Precisely 2–3 in the majors

Over a 3◇ rebid the responder may seek a 4–4 fit by introducing a 4-card major of his own.

Here are two sequences using the convention:

West	*East*	*West*	*East*
♠KJ3	♠Q1062	2NT	3♣
♡AQJ54	♡K83	3♡	4♡
◇A2	◇8753	End	
♣KQ5	♣92		

Had West's response been 3◇, East would have continued with 3♠, seeking a 4–4 fit in that suit. As you see, 3NT would have been at risk on a minor suit lead.

West	*East*	*West*	*East*
♠AQ92	♠KJ54	2NT	3♣
♡K4	♡Q972	3◇	3♡
◇AKJ3	◇752	3♠	4♠
♣A104	♣93	End	

West denies a 5-card major but the 4–4 spade fit comes to light.

Responder is 5–4 in the majors

When responder has 5 hearts and 4 spades there is no problem. He starts with 3♡, expecting the opener to show a 4-card spade suit if he cannot support the hearts.

The situation is slightly more awkward when responder has 5 spades and 4 hearts. He must start with 3♣, 5-card Stayman. If opener makes the special response of 3NT, showing 2 spades and 3 hearts, then there is no 8-card fit. After the alternative sequence of 2NT – 3♣ – 3◇ – 3♡ – 3NT, responder can be sure that there is a 5–3 spade fit.

Assessment. There is little to choose between Five-card Stayman and its main rival, Baron. Baron cannot detect a 5–3 major fit but makes it easier to uncover 4–4 fits in a minor.

FLANNERY TWO DIAMONDS

This convention is an opening bid used on hands containing (at any rate in its original form) precisely four spades and five hearts, usually in the 11–15 range. A response of 2NT is forcing. Opener then rebids 3♣ or 3♢ with three cards in the suit named, 3♡ on a minimum 4–5–2–2, 3♠ on a maximum with this shape.

Assessment.   Flannery has never been much played in Britain, but it has had a long life in America. However, it seems to us a very poor use for 2♢, since 4–5 major-suit hands are easy to manage by natural methods.

FORCING 1NT RESPONSE

In systems which employ 5-card major openings, such as Precision, a response of 1NT to 1♡ or 1♠ is generally played as forcing (unless responder is a passed hand). If the opener is 5–3–3–2 he will rebid in a 3-card minor (2♣ with three cards in both minors).

Assessment.   There are many advantages in this scheme. For example, responder can raise the opener's suit to the three level in two ways, either directly or via a 1NT response. The latter sequence would suggest a flattish hand with only 3-card trump support. It is true that the partnership can settle in 1NT less often, but to play in two of a major with a 5–2 combination is hardly a disaster.

FORCING PASS

This phrase describes occasions where a player passes in a forcing situation, leaving the next move to his partner. It is a familiar tactic at high levels, where the stronger side may have to decide whether to double their opponents' sacrifice or bid one more themselves.

At game to North–South the bidding goes:

South	West	North	East
1♠	2♡	4♠	5♡
?			

South holds: ♠ AKJ83   ♡ A5   ◇ KJ72   ♣ J9

From South's point of view there is a fair chance that his side can make eleven tricks. He makes a forcing pass, leaving the decision to his partner. The pass is forcing because it can hardly be right, having bid to a vulnerable game, to let the opponents play undoubled at the five level.

A pass in a forcing situation may be good tactics also at lower levels. For example:

South	West	North	East
1♡	No	2♣	2◇
?			

South holds: ♠ AJ5   ♡ KJ973   ◇ A8   ♣ Q62

South has enough for 2♡ or 3♣, but it is better tactics to pass and await partner's action. Having responded at the two level, North will certainly not allow the opponents to play in 2◇.

Assessment. When there is doubt, a forcing pass has a way of being better than any of the alternatives. In the second sequence above, either 2♡ or 3♣ would be limited bids and might be passed.

FOUR NO-TRUMP OPENING

On certain, somewhat rare, hands you can tell what the best contract will be just by asking partner to name any ace he may hold. You do this by opening with a 4NT call. The responses are:

5♣	no ace
5◇/5♡/5♠	the ace of that suit
5NT	two aces
6♣	the ace of clubs

So, suppose you were fortunate to pick up this collection:

♠ AKQJ872   ♡ KQJ93   ◇ A   ♣ −

You would open 4NT. If partner responded 5♣ (no ace) or 6♣ (ace of clubs) you would stop in 6♠. Over a 5♡ response you would bid 7♠; over 5NT you would go to 7NT.

Assessment.   The convention is especially useful when you hold a void and standard Blackwood responses would be no use. A once-a-year treat, it is true.

FREE BID, RAISE, OR REBID

A free bid, raise, or rebid is a bid made over intervention when the alternative was to pass.

A free raise, in a sequence such as

South	*West*	*North*	*East*
1♡	2♣	2♡	

used to imply better than a minimum raise (on the grounds that South would in any case get another chance). This style has rightly been left on the back-burner. It is poor tactics not to raise when the opportunity is present; if you pass, you lay yourself open to pre-emptive action by East, the fourth player.

Similarly, a free bid in a sequence such as

South	*West*	*North*	*East*
1◇	1♡	1♠	

nowadays implies no more general values than the same call made without intervention. It is true that it implies a better *suit*; you would not make such a call on a 6-count with Jxxx in spades.

Similarly, a free rebid in the opener's suit, such as

South	West	North	East
1♣	Pass	1♡	1♠
2♣			

means what it says, a limited hand with good clubs. If South's clubs were not particularly noteworthy, such as K10xxx, he would pass.

Assessment. The modern tendency, as you see, is to indicate limited values when space permits, particularly when you have a fit for partner. When you can be sure that the bidding will continue, and you have nothing special to say, it is usually good tactics to pass.

GERBER CONVENTION

In this convention 4♣ takes the place of Blackwood as a form of ace inquiry. The responses are:

4♢	0 or 3 aces
4♡	1 or 4 aces
4♠	2 aces

Even players who normally use Blackwood sometimes substitute Gerber opposite an opening 1NT or 2NT. Suppose your partner opens 1NT and you hold:

♠ KQ10854   ♡ 5   ♢ AKQ4   ♣ K3

The response to a Gerber 4♣ will tell you where you stand.

When you need to ask for kings subsequently you may bid 5♣, with similar responses to those for the ace-ask.

Assessment. On many occasions Gerber in place of Blackwood will save a 'leg' in the bidding; but whether this compensates for the loss of 4♣ where this would be a valuable cue bid is dubious. For players who make good use of cue bids in their slam sequences, Gerber is best restricted to when partner has opened 1NT or 2NT.

GRAND SLAM TRY

The original grand slam force was the Josephine (Culbertson) 5NT. A bid of 5NT, when not preceded by a Blackwood 4NT, directs partner to bid seven of the agreed trump suit if he holds two of the three top honours.

This would be a typical auction:

West	East	West	East
♠KJ5	♠—	1♡	3◇
♡AQ10764	♡K92	3♡	5NT
◇63	◇AKQ952	7♡	End
♣Q8	♣A1073		

When the trump suit is a major, it is possible to lay out a more detailed scale of responses to 5NT:

6♣	Ace or king
6◇	Queen
6 trump suit	No top honour
7 trump suit	Two top honours

Over 6♣ the enquirer may bid 6◇, asking partner to bid seven if he holds an extra trump. This allows you to bid a grand with a trump holding such as AJxxx opposite Kxxxx.

Assessment.   Since the advent of Roman Key Card Blackwood (where the responses involve the king and queen of the intended trump suit), there is less need for grand slam tries centred on the trump honours. The 5NT call is still useful when you hold a void, as in the example above; Blackwood responses would then be unhelpful.

HERBERT RESPONSES

A Herbert response is one where the 'next suit up' is artificial and denotes weakness. (2◇ over 2♣, though not described as Herbert, is an example). Some Italian systems use the cheapest response to a take-out double in this way.

The principle use nowadays is as a negative response to a strong two bid. Playing Herbert responses, the responder shows a negative by bidding 2♡ over 2◇, 2♠ over 2♡, and 3♣ over 2♠. You save space in many sequences (as compared with the normal negative of 2NT).

When you hold a positive response in the next suit up you bid 2NT. So, 2◇ – 2NT would show a positive in hearts.

Assessment. Herbert responses are surely good medicine when replying to a forcing two bid of any kind.

INVERTED MINOR SUIT RAISES

It is quite common in tournament play to reverse the meanings of a single raise of a minor suit and a double raise. Then 1◇ – 2◇ becomes stronger than 1◇ – 3◇ and is played as forcing (unless responder is a passed hand). The intention is two fold: to provide a forcing raise in a minor (a notable gap in standard methods), and to shut out the enemy when you have a good fit and a relatively weak hand.

Assessment. This is a sensible idea, particularly in tournament play where competition for part scores is fierce and opponents would rarely pass out a standard 1◇ – 2◇ auction.

JUMP CUE-BID OVERCALLS

What meaning should be given to an overcall of 3♣ over an opponent's 1♣ opening, or 3♠ over a 1♠ opening? In a minor there is some sense in saying that the jump overcall should be natural, since the opening may be based on a short suit. This makes no sense when a major suit is involved and the meaning normally attributed is

'Have you a stop in the enemy suit? If so, bid 3NT.'

♠ 7   ♡ A8   ◇ AKQ10742   ♣ K93

Holding this hand you would call 3♠ over an opponent's 1♠ opening.

Assessment. In the old days, when psyching was not regarded as sinful, even 3♠ over 1♠ would be played as natural. Nowadays the interpretation above makes more sense.

JUMP OVERCALLS

Jump overcalls, both weak and strong, are discussed in Chapter 11.

LEAD-DIRECTING DOUBLE

Enemy auctions, particularly slam auctions, give many opportunities for a lead-directing double by the defenders. Suppose the auction starts like this:

West	North	East	South
2♠	Pass	4♠	Pass
5♣	Pass	5◇	Dble

South's double of the control-showing cue bid suggests that partner should lead a diamond.

Just as important are the occasions when a defender does *not* double.

West	North	East	South
1◇	Pass	2♠	Pass
3♠	Pass	4NT	Pass
5♡	Pass	6♠	End

South will take note of North's pass over 5♡. This may incline South towards a lead of the other unbid suit, clubs.

Assessment. Such doubles make good sense when the aim is to attract a promising opening lead. It is foolish to double artificial bids in other situations – when you hold such as Q10xxxx in the suit, or when you yourself will be on lead. This type of double serves only to give valuable information to declarer.

LEBENSOHL CONVENTION

Suppose your partner opens 1NT and the next player overcalls 2♠. You might now want to compete in a suit, without inviting partner to bid on. You might instead want to make a forcing call in some suit. The Lebensohl convention allows you to make this distinction.

A response of 2NT (over 2♡ or 2♠ intervention) is a transfer to 3♣; the responder may now make various continuations, thereby almost doubling the number of sequences at his disposal. Suppose the bidding starts:

South	West	North	East
1NT	2♠	?	

North has these options:

Double	Shows initially the values for a raise to 2NT (without guaranteeing values in spades), but may be stronger
2NT	Tells opener to rebid 3♣. Responder may then pass or bid 3♢ or 3♡, both simply competitive
3♣/3♢/3♡	All forcing
3♠	Staymanic, indicating four hearts, also promising a spade guard
3NT	To play, again promising a spade guard

In addition, responder may make the 3♠ and 3NT calls via the Lebensohl 2NT transfer. Both these sequences deny a guard in the enemy suit.

When the overcall is 2♡ responder has one extra bid at his disposal and the scheme becomes:

2♠	simply competitive
2NT, then 3♠	invitational
3♠	forcing

Other bids have the same sense as above.

Lebensohl may be used also over artificial 2♣ and 2♢ overcalls, such as Astro.

Assessment.   Playing Lebensohl, you cannot double for penalties (although partner may pass your double) or bid a natural 2NT. On the other hand, the convention greatly increases the number of sequences available. In the tournament world it is widely played . . . by those who have good memories, anyway!

LIGHTNER DOUBLE

A double of a slam contract (unless this is an obvious sacrifice) is usually played as lead-directing, requesting an 'unusual' lead. Suppose the bidding goes:

South	West	North	East
1♠	No	3♠	4♣
6♠	No	No	Dble
End			

East is saying, 'Don't lead my suit or a harmless trump.' He probably has a void or possibly an AK in one of the red suits. This type of double is known as a *Lightner Double*.

A double of a freely bid 3NT contract is also, as a rule, lead-directing. If the doubler has overcalled in a suit he is demanding the lead of this suit. If the player on lead has overcalled, and his partner has remained silent, the double requests that the suit of the overcall be led nevertheless. In cases where the defenders have not bid, the double usually shows strength in dummy's main suit.

Occasionally such a double is made when the auction has been a simple 1NT – 3NT. The message then is 'I have a good, perhaps solid, suit somewhere. Please try to find it rather than lead your own best suit'.

Assessment. The Lightner slam double is a weapon carried by all good players. As for doubles of 3NT, among good players there is a move away from the orthodoxies described above. The doubler says 'I think we can beat it; use your head.'

LOWER MINOR CONVENTION

The idea is to play 3♦ over an opening 3♣ as a request for take-out, and 4♣ as the take-out request over any other Three bids.

Assessment. Anything more inept than bidding 4♣ as a take-out over 3♦ or 3♡ is difficult to imagine. Nevertheless, the convention has had a long life and still lingers in some places.

MICHAELS CUE BID

In the old days an overcall in the opponent's suit, such as 2♦ over 1♦, showed an enormous take-out double. This was a poor idea on two grounds: the opportunities for such a call were infrequent; and the giant hands could be adequately managed by starting with a double.

In the Michaels scheme a cue bid shows a moderate two-suiter including any unbid majors:

2♣ over 1♣ (or 2♦ over 1♦)	shows both majors, at least 5–4

2♡ over 1♡   shows spades and a minor, at least 5–5

2♠ over 1♠   shows hearts and a minor, at least 5–5

At favourable vulnerability a Michaels cue bid may be made on quite a modest hand:

(1)   ♠ KJ94   ♡ AJ1052   ◇ 104   ♣ 83

Here you would make the appropriate cue bid over a 1♣ or 1◇ opening.

Sometimes you will be much stronger:

(2)   ♠ AKJ76   ♡ KQJ62   ◇ K8   ♣ 4

This is well above the normal strength for a Michaels call, so after a start of 1◇ – 2◇ – Pass – 2♡; Pass – ?, you would advance to 3♡, indicating your power.

A major-suit Michaels bid may carry the bidding to the three level and should therefore be based on a hand with fair playing strength.

(3)   ♠ K10753   ♡ A4   ◇ KQ973   ♣ 6

On this you say 2♡ over 1♡. If partner has no support for spades and wishes to discover your minor, he responds 2NT.

New suits by the responder to Michaels are non-forcing and evidently display a powerful suit, not less than QJ10xxx. The only forcing response is a repeat cue bid in the enemy suit.

Assessment.   Michaels is a good convention when the hand is strong enough to present reasonable hopes of challenging for the contract. Since holding both majors is a good start in this direction, a 2♣ or 2◇ Michaels bid does not require the same values as an Unusual No-trump overcall. Nevertheless, it is unwise to wave an arm feebly in the air every time you hold 5–4 shape and 7 or 8 points. This is simply a gift to the opposition.

MINOR-SUIT SWISS

This convention is designed to cover a small deficiency in standard systems. Suppose partner opens 1◇ and you hold:

♠ AQ5   ♡ 62   ◇ AQ754   ♣ J105

A raise to 3◇ would be non-forcing. In the absence of any convention, you would have to choose between an 'invented' 2♣ bid and a leap to 3NT, trusting partner for the heart stop.

Minor-suit Swiss involves two conventional responses to one of a minor:

3♡   strong support for the minor, plus a good heart stop
3♠   strong support for the minor, plus a good spade stop

So, on the hand above you would respond 3♠, leaving partner to judge the best spot. These responses are forcing to game, so if partner's next move is to call four of his minor he is inviting you to cue bid.

Assessment. The traditional leaps to 3♡ and 3♠, indicating a weak hand with a long suit, are dispensable. Minor-suit Swiss certainly helps you bid more accurately but may on occasion help the defenders with their opening lead, particularly when the Swiss call is doubled. If your hand is fairly flat there is a lot to be said for the old-fashioned direct 3NT call.

MULTI-COLOURED TWO DIAMONDS

An opening 2◇ is enrolled to cover five different types of hand:

(a)   a weak two in hearts
(b)   a weak two in spades
(c)   a balanced 19–20 count
(d)   a strong two in clubs
(e)   a strong two in diamonds

The responder assumes initially that the bid is based on one of the weak types. These options are open to him:

2♡   'If you have a weak 2♡ let's play there'
2♠   'This is high enough if you have a weak 2♠; I am willing to go higher in hearts'
2NT   'What type do you have?'
        Opener now rebids:
        3♣ – upper range with hearts
        3♢ – upper range with spades
        3♡ – lower range with hearts
        3♠ – lower range with spades
        3NT – balanced 19–20 points
        4♣/4♢ – strong two
3 any   Forcing

When the opener holds one of the strong types he rebids in obvious fashion opposite a 2♡ or 2♠ response (2NT on 19–20, 3♣/3♢ with a strong minor).

Here are two typical auctions:

West	East	West	East
♠AJ10752	♠K963	2♢	2♡
♡64	♡A3	2♠	3♠
♢108	♢KQJ5	4♠	End
♣K73	♣Q104		

East sees no future facing a weak two in hearts but makes a game try when partner shows that his Multi is based on a spade suit. West happily accepts the try.

West	East	West	East
♠KQ9752	♠AJ72	2◇	2NT
♡Q9	♡J6	3◇	4♣
◇Q105	◇AK8	4♠	End
♣83	♣AK97		

West shows an upper-range weak two in spades and East's 4♣ is a cue bid. (East cannot have a massive club suit because with that hand he would have responded 3♣ instead of 2NT). West's 4♠ call denies any controls in the red suits and East now knows that there are two losers in hearts.

Since weak-two types are covered by the Multi, opening bids of 2♡ and 2♠ become strong (Acol-type). 2♣ holds its traditional (super-strong) meaning and 2NT indicates 21–22.

Defence to the Multi

The Multi is easy to play, not so easy to defend against. This scheme is probably best:

> 1. *Action by second hand.* Double is 13–17 flattish, or any distributional 18+ hand; 2♡/2♠ are natural; 2NT is about 16–19, stops in both majors.
>
> 2. *Action by fourth hand after 2◇ – Pass – 2♡.* 2♠ and 2NT are natural; double is a take-out of hearts or any powerful hand. With short spades you wait for the expected 2♠ rebid, then enter with a take-out double on the next round.
>
> 3. *Action by fourth hand after 2◇ – Pass – 2♠.* Now double is a take-out double of spades (likely to be the opener's suit).

Assessment. Although the Multi (first so named by one of the present authors) is famed for creating problems for the opponents, many people overlook its main advantage – it is economical in the sense that it covers various types with one bid. Compare the somewhat feeble Flannery Two Diamonds.

NEGATIVE DOUBLE

In a sequence such as $1\diamondsuit - 1\spadesuit - $ Dble, the double is traditionally for penalties. This is hopelessly inefficient, warning the opponents of danger at much too low a level. Even if the doubler has a strong hand and $1\spadesuit$ goes a couple down he will surely find that he could have made 3NT.

In the tournament world, at any rate, such doubles of overcalls are played for take-out. They are then called Negative Doubles (or Sputnik Doubles, since they originated at the time of the first Russian satellite). This would be a typical hand for such a double:

North	South	West	North	East
$\spadesuit$J6	$1\diamondsuit$	$1\spadesuit$	Dble	
$\heartsuit$AQ52				
$\diamondsuit$874				
$\clubsuit$Q1065				

North's negative double means 'I have the values to bid but no good bid to make'. It suggests initially about 7–10 points but may be based on a stronger hand. Suppose that East passes, after the above start, and South holds one of these hands:

(1)	$\spadesuit$Q5	(2)	$\spadesuit$K932
	$\heartsuit$K943		$\heartsuit$74
	$\diamondsuit$AQ1063		$\diamondsuit$AK95
	$\clubsuit$J3		$\clubsuit$A84

On (1) South bids $2\heartsuit$, on (2) he bids 1NT, expecting his partner to hold values in hearts.

The negative doubler may pass these rebids. If he advances in some other direction the inference will be that he has reserves of strength.

When negative doubles are being played a cue bid by responder will indicate a fit for the opener's suit.

Suppose the auction starts like this

South	West	North	East
1◇	1♠	?	

and, as North, you hold this hand:

♠ 93   ♡ AQ6   ◇ KQ1092   ♣ Q74

You cue-bid 2♠, showing a game-forcing hand with good diamond support. Clearly, when the fit is in a minor, you are hoping that partner can bid no-trumps.

A cue bid facing a major-suit opening (1♠ – 2♣ – 3♣) indicates a hand worth at least a sound game raise.

The level of negative doubles

Some players use negative doubles only when there has been a 1♠ overcall. Most tournament players, though, use them against any overcall up to the level of 3♡ or 3♠. You may also encounter theorists (in the worst sense of the word) who regard such as 1◇ – 4♠ – Dble as an invitation to further action!

Action when strong in the enemy suit

Since a penalty double is not available you have to pass on many hands where you would have been happy to wield the stick.

North	South	West	North	East
♠76	1♠	2◇	?	
♡J2				
◇AJ84				
♣A10652				

Here you might fancy your chances of punishing 2◇. Playing negative doubles you have to pass. If East passes also there is a good chance that South will re-open the auction with a take-out double, not wishing to sell out at such a low level. You can then pass this call for penalties.

Assessment.   Negative doubles are an important part of the modern game, where opponents will seize any opportunity to rob you of bidding space. There are also some valuable inferences that arise from the negative double. For example, what do you make of North's call here?

South	West	North	East
1♢	1♡	1♠	

North would have used a negative double if he held only four spades, so now he shows five spades (or four very good ones, such as AKJ10).

NEW SUIT RESPONSE NON-FORCING AFTER INTERVENTION

Suppose the bidding starts 1♢ – 1♠ – ? and you find yourself staring at:

♠ 93   ♡ AQJ742   ♢ 53   ♣ J104

You would like to bid 2♡ if you knew the bidding could stop there; unfortunately in standard methods such a call would be forcing and therefore somewhat unsound.

One of the advantages of playing negative doubles (*see* above) is that you *can* make such calls in a new suit non-forcing. This is the scheme:

New suit (of higher rank)	non-forcing
Double, then new suit	forcing

So, on the above hand you could bid 2♡ immediately and partner would place you with about 7–10 points and a good suit. Give yourself the ace of clubs as well and you would be too good for a (non-forcing) 2♡ bid. You would start with a negative double, intending to introduce the hearts on the next round.

Assessment.   This is surely the right method when responder's suit is *higher* than the suit of the opening bid, as in the example above.

Most players limit the treatment only to those occasions. In an auction such as 1♢ – 1♠ – 2♣, where the response is in a lower suit than the opener's, responder's call would be forcing.

OPTIONAL DOUBLE

A double of a pre-emptive opening is sometimes described as 'optional', requiring partner to pass or take out according to the nature of his hand.

♠ AQJ3   ♡ 94   ♢ A8   ♣ KQ1075

Here you would like to make a genuinely optional double over 3♡.

Assessment. This style of double is no longer at all common. Players still talk about 'optional doubles' but up to the level of 4♢ they generally mean 'primarily for take-out'.

PRINCIPLE OF FAST ARRIVAL

This phrase relates to occasions when the partners are committed to reaching game and one of them goes directly to game, spurning the chance to investigate a slam by making a forcing call at a lower level. The inference is that he is not interested in a slam. An example occurs in a partnership sequence such as 1♠ – 2♢, 3♢ – 5♢. The 5♢ bidder had room to make a cue bid in hearts or clubs; his chosen call means 'I think we might make this, but there is no need to investigate slam possibilities'.

Similarly a sequence such as 1♡ – 2♠ – 4♠ would carry the message 'I have good spade support but a minimum hand'. If the opener were stronger he would bid 3♠ for the moment, leaving room for his partner to make a cue bid. The jump to 4♠ suggests a hand such as:

♠ KJ84   ♡ AQJ92   ♢ 103   ♣ J5

Assessment. The idea is sound, especially in a negative sense. When a player spurns an opportunity to make a 'fast arrival' bid, he indicates that he is better than minimum and interested in various possibilities.

PSYCHIC BIDDING

A psychic bid is one where the object is to mislead the opposition, giving a false picture of your holding. For example, you might open 1♠ on:

♠ 982   ♡ J1065   ◇ QJ10762   ♣ –

Such out-and-out psyches played a part in the game a few decades ago. Now they have largely died out, partly because of an improvement in the general standard of bidding, partly because of a war waged on them by the bridge authorities. There is still plenty of scope, though, for a gentler type of psyche – where the bidder may have good values but chooses to show a suit or a control that he does not hold.

♠ AQ8   ♡ KJ10   ◇ A942   ♣ 974

Partner opens 1◇. Expecting to end in 3NT and fearful of a club lead, you respond 2♣.

The psychic cue bid is another favourite:

♠ AKJ872   ♡ 4   ◇ AQ65   ♣ 72

Partner opens the bidding and you soon agree spades as trumps. Now may be the moment for a psychic cue bid in clubs, hoping to deter a club lead.

Perhaps the most common type of psyche occurs in this situation. Partner opens 1♡ and the next player makes a take-out double. You hold:

♠ 76   ♡ Q1093   ◇ K53   ♣ K842

At some levels of play you may find it effective to bid 1♠ now, trying to rob the opponents of their likely fit in that suit. The best counter to such tactics is for the fourth player to make a penalty double of 1♠ whenever he holds four cards in the suit and upwards of 7 points or so. When the spade bidder retreats to hearts the defenders may investigate a spade contract.

When partner opens with some weak call and you yourself have a poor hand, a show of strength may inconvenience the enemy. Suppose that partner opens 3◇, non-vulnerable, and the next player passes. You hold:

    ♠ J82   ♡ 107   ◇ K942   ♣ KJ75

You can try the effect of a 3♠ response. If the next player has some hand that is 5–4 in the majors, his entry into the auction will be decidedly more awkward than if you had passed or raised the diamonds.

Assessment.   Psychic bids are unlikely to achieve a brilliant result, but like a bluff at poker they create an air of uncertainty. If you acquire a reputation for the occasional 'tricky' bid you may gain when the opponents incorrectly suspect you of some mischief.

QUANTITATIVE 4NT

For some players 4NT is a fixed light in the heavens – Blackwood unless it can be proved otherwise to judge and jury. It is more sensible to define occasions when the bid should be interpreted as natural:

1.   When no genuine suit has been mentioned, as in a sequence such as 1NT – 2♣ – 2◇ – 4NT. The responder is asking his partner to bid 6NT unless he is minimum.

2.   When no trump suit has been agreed and the previous call was in no-trumps, such as 1♠ – 2◇ – 2NT – 4NT. An exception to this is when the responder made a jump shift: 1♠ – 3♡ – 3NT – 4NT. Here the responder had no room to confirm the suit and 4NT should be taken as Blackwood.

3.   When a player has made a natural, limited, bid in no-trumps and partner advances in a suit, suggesting a slam, a minimum bid of 4NT is natural: 1♠ – 2♣ – 3NT – 4♣ – 4NT. The opener has an unexciting 18-count, unsuitable for slam play.

Assessment.   You will hear some players say 'When I bid 4NT, whatever the auction, I want to know how many aces you've got'. They are lopping off half the value of the call.

RESPONSIVE DOUBLE

When an opening bid is doubled, third hand raises the opener's suit, and fourth hand doubles, the final double is usually not for penalties. It conveys the message 'I have the values to make a call but no particularly good suit to bid'. It asks the doubler to suggest a suit.

South	*West*	*North*	*East*
1♠	Dble	2♠	Dble

East holds: ♠ 65   ♡ J86   ◇ KJ73   ♣ Q1052

Such doubles are primarily for take-out up to the level of three spades. At the four level, in an auction such as

South	*West*	*North*	*East*
1◇	Dble	4◇	Dble

the second double would still be responsive, showing general values rather than a trick in diamonds. However, West might well leave in the double unless his own hand was particularly distributional.

Assessment.   Responsive doubles are almost universal in tournament bridge and popular even at rubber bridge. They make good sense because it is rarely profitable at a low level to penalise opponents who have found a fit.

RIPSTRA DEFENCE TO 1NT

Most defences to 1NT are aimed at locating a major-suit fit. This makes good sense because with a minor-suit fit you will often be outbid by the opponents. The Ripstra Defence uses these two calls artificially (both in 2nd and 4th seat):

2♣	both majors and better clubs than diamonds
2♢	both majors and better diamonds than clubs

(1)	♠KQ54	(2)	♠AJ43	(3)	♠K10965
	♡A1093		♡KQ742		♡AJ943
	♢8		♢J83		♢K3
	♣A842		♣Q		♣7

Hand (1) would justify 2♣ over the opening 1NT, on (2) 2♢ would be best. Reluctant to be shut out on (3) you might risk a 2♢ bid, hoping that partner would not choose to pass.

Partner, of course, is free to pass the Ripstra call (or to bid 2♢ over 2♣) when his length is in that area.

Assessment. The method works well when you hold a suitable hand, but the three-suiters for which it is devised are not that common. *See Astro* for what is nowadays a more popular method.

ROMAN KEY CARD BLACKWOOD

Here, as in Five-ace Blackwood, the king of trumps is counted as an ace. The responses to Roman Key Card Blackwood involve the queen of trumps too:

5♣	0 or 3 'aces' (the trump king counting as an ace)
5♢	1 or 4 'aces'
5♡	2 'aces' without the trump queen
5♠	2 'aces' with the trump queen

After a 5♣ or 5 ♢ response the Blackwood bidder may inquire about the trump queen by bidding five of the 'nearest' suit (other than trumps). The opener then signs off in the trump suit when lacking the trump queen, cue-bids a king or bids no-trumps when possessing the trump queen (or perhaps greater length than he has so far shown).

The 4NT bidder has various other moves open to him on the next round:

5NT	asks responder how many side-suit kings he holds (6♣ = 0, 6♢ = 1, etc.)
New suit	(when not the trump-queen enquiry mentioned above) asks for a second-round control of the suit bid. Responder bids seven with the control.

Here is an example of the second-round control enquiry:

West	East	West	East
♠AQJ8742	♠K106	2♠	3♠
♡AQ4	♡9	4♣	4♢
♢K2	♢A974	4NT	5♡
♣A	♣J8752	6♡	7♠
		End	

East's 5♡ response shows two of the five 'aces'. West asks about second-round heart control and East admits to this with a leap to the grand slam.

Assessment.   This style of Blackwood lacks the simplicity of other approaches but at this level a little hard work is justified. Counting the king of trumps as an ace increases the chance that a disappointing response will carry you past the safe level, particularly when clubs are trumps.

SHORT SUIT GAME TRIES

After a sequence such as 1♡ – 2♡ we saw in Chapter 3 that it was normal for the opener to bid three of his longest side suit to invite a game. Using 'short suit game tries' the opener instead shows his shortest side suit, usually a singleton. Responder can then tell if he has values wasted in that quarter. A holding of xxx, Jxxx, or Axxx would be good news, something like KJxx would very likely be bad news.

Assessment. On a particular hand it is a question of luck whether long-suit or short-suit tries work better. The fact that responder's trumps are usually shorter than the opener's, and that ruffs in his hand will therefore be more productive, appears to give the edge to long-suit game tries; on the other hand the try that specifically names a singleton is more precise.

SNAP

The initials stand for Strong No-trump After Passing and the idea is that a 1NT response by a passed hand should show around 9–12 points. This keeps the auction under control when the player in third or fourth seat has opened light. The 2NT response becomes idle and can be used to show a super raise to three in the opener's suit.

For a similar method *see* the *Drury Convention*.

Assessment. The convention works well when responder has a hand in the 9–12 point range. He will not be so happy when he has 7–8 points and partner opens one of a major. The choice then will be between a strangled pass and a stretch to the SNAP 1NT.

SOS REDOUBLE

When you redouble a game or slam contract the message is clear – you think the contract can be made. In general, when you redouble a part score that has been doubled for penalties the message is the opposite. You are saying to partner 'I don't like this very much – try another spot'. This would be a typical 'SOS Redouble':

West	North	East	South
1♡	2♣	Dble	Rdble

South holds

♠ Q10762   ♡ J7   ◇ J96532   ♣ –

and hopes that one of his suits will prove a safer resting spot.

Sometimes the player who made the call that has been doubled may initiate a rescue.

West	North	East	South
1♣	Dble	Pass	Pass
Rdble			

West, who knows that South has a stack of clubs, holds:

♠ AQ8   ♡ KJ6   ◇ Q92   ♣ J842

Obviously one club doubled is unbearable.

It is sometimes possible to bid a non-existent suit, in the expectation that you will be doubled and can then redouble for rescue.

West	North	East	South
1NT	Dble	?	

East, after the above auction, holds

♠ Q10873   ♡ J9542   ◇ 86   ♣ 3

When non-vulnerable, he may try the effect of 2◇. If this bid is doubled he will redouble, asking partner to choose a major. Opponents nowadays tend to be alert to this manoeuvre and quite happy to pass and pick up a bundle of 50s.

Only when the doubled bid is in no-trumps is a redouble of a part score played for business:

West	North	East	South
1♡	1NT	Dble	Rdble

Here South flings back the challenge, expressing confidence in his partner's prospects.

Assessment.   Redoubles in the sense that we have described above are widely played in tournament bridge. This makes good sense because making a doubled part score will usually give you an excellent score anyway.

SOUTH AFRICAN TEXAS OPENING

Natural minor-suit openings at the four level are dispensable and many pairs prefer to use such calls to indicate upper-range pre-empts in a major. Playing South African Texas, 4♣ shows a strong 4♡ opening, 4♢ shows a strong 4♠ opening.

♠ AKQJ863   ♡ Q5   ♢ K103   ♣ 6

On this hand you would open 4♢ to show a strong pre-empt in spades. Make ♢K a small card and you would open 4♠ instead.

The responder to 4♣ or 4♢ may show interest in a slam by bidding the intermediate suit (for example, 4♢ over 4♣); such a call is artificial and does not necessarily show a control in the suit bid.

Assessment.   As well as distinguishing between two types of four-level pre-empt, a Texas opening usually allows the unknown hand to become declarer.

SPLINTER BID

A splinter is a jump bid that indicates a side-suit shortage. Look at
the three sequences 1♠ – 2♣; 1♠ – 3♣; 1♠ – 4♣. In the first two
the responding call is needed in a natural sense. This is not so in the
third, so 4♣ may be played as a splinter, agreeing spades as trumps
and showing a singleton or void club.

West	East	West	East
♠AQ1086	♠KJ53	1♠	4♣
♡K8	♡AJ76	4♠	End
◇J74	◇A962		
♣KQ8	♣6		

East shows a good raise to game including a singleton club. West
has fair values but knows that his KQx in clubs will be wasted
opposite a singleton; he signs off. Had West's minor suits been the
other way round his next move would have been 4NT.

Since the four-level responses are all used as splinter bids, some
other call is needed to announce a sound game raise that does not
include a singleton or void. One idea, although rubber bridge
players may not care for the suggestion, is to use 3NT for this
purpose.

Splinter bids may be used also on auctions such as: 1♠ – 2♡ – 4♣.
A rebid of 3♣ would be forcing, so 4♣ is a splinter bid, agreeing
hearts as trumps and showing a shortage in clubs.

Assessment.   Splinter bids are a useful way of conveying two kinds
of information in a single call. When used opposite openings of 1♡
and 1♠ they are a rival scheme to the *Swiss Convention* (*see* later).

SPUTNIK DOUBLES

See Negative Double.

STAYMAN OPPOSITE 1NT OVERCALL

We looked at the basic Stayman convention in Chapter 4. The same
convention may be used when partner has overcalled 1NT.

South	West	North	East
1◇	1NT	No	2♣

East's call asks partner if he holds a 4-card major. If the partnership uses transfer responses to a 1NT opening, they may be used in this situation too. 2◇ would request a transfer to 2♡, 2♡ a transfer to 2♠.

Assessment.   The use of Stayman (and transfer bids) can be as useful opposite a 1NT overcall as opposite a 1NT opening. Also, it is easier on the memory to use the same scheme in both situations.

SWISS CONVENTION

When partner opens 1♡ or 1♠ hands worth a raise to game are of various types, some defensive and some containing fair values. In the Swiss Convention responses of 4♣ and 4◇ are enlisted to describe the stronger types. There are many variants but this one, known as Fruit Machine Swiss, is popular and efficient:

4♣	shows two aces plus (a) a singleton, or
	(b) the king of trumps, or
	(c) a third ace
4◇	shows a sound raise to game lacking the requirements for 4♣

Following a 4♣ response the opener may enquire with 4◇. The responder then bids his singleton on (a) even if it carries him beyond game, four of the trump suit on (b), and 4NT on (c).

Assessment.   Swiss, or some convention like it, is very necessary to distinguish the types shown above from pre-emptive raises that may contain very few high cards. For a different method, where a short side suit is named immediately, *see* Splinter Bids.

THREE NO-TRUMP OPENING

Since very strong balanced hands can be expressed by a sequence such as 2♣ – 2♦ – 3NT, there has long been a convention whereby an *opening* 3NT should be a form of pre-empt, based on a solid minor suit and not more than a queen outside. When this style of 3NT is played, responder may bid 4♣ if unwilling to let 3NT stand; opener will then pass or convert to 4♦. A response of 4♦ is conventional, asking opener to show a singleton (4NT will deny one, five of the trump suit will show a singleton in the other minor). A response of 5♣ is to play at game level in partner's minor.

Assessment. A sparkling success in 3NT, bid and made, is not the main object. The 3NT opening is (a) pre-emptive and (b) often places a minor-suit declaration in the unknown hand. Against that, it is not uncommon for 3NT to be played by the wrong hand, with the lead coming through an unprotected king in dummy.

TRANSFER BIDS

Transfer responses to a 1NT opening are more or less universal in the tournament world. It is possible to play simply that 2♦ over 1NT shows a heart suit and 2♥ a spade suit, but most partnerships take it further than that. This is the scheme of responses recommended by the authors in *Acol in the 90s* (Robert Hale):

2♦	transfer to hearts
2♥	transfer to spades
2♠	Baron, asking for 4-card suits (shown upwards)
2NT	transfer to 3♣; responder may then pass or bid 3♦ (weak); a continuation such as 3♥ would mean both minors and short hearts
3♣/3♦	invitational on a 6-card suit
3♥/3♠	pre-emptive

These are typical sequences:

(1)	*West*	*East*	(2)	*West*	*East*
	1NT	2♦		1NT	2♡
	2♡	2NT		2♠	3♦

In (1) East shows a limit raise to 2NT that includes a 5-card heart suit. In (2) East has five spades and at least four diamonds; the sequence is forcing to 3♠. A jump rebid of 4♦ by East would have shown a big two-suiter, spades and diamonds.

Since immediate three-level responses to 1NT are non-forcing (*see* above), such responses via Stayman are forcing.

(3)	*West*	*East*	(4)	*West*	*East*
	1NT	2♣		1NT	2♣
	2♠	3♣		2♦	3♠

In (3) East's 3♣ is game-forcing; he may hold four hearts. Similarly, in (4) East's 3♠ is game-forcing.

Breaking transfer bids

When the 1NT opener has strong support for the suit proposed by his partner he is free to make a jump in the suit. Say that you open a 12–14 1NT on:

♠ K5   ♡ A1084   ♦ Q73   ♣ AJ85

If partner responds 2♡ you say 2♠. If he responds 2♦, though, it cannot be wrong to jump to 3♡. If you go one down, this will surely be saving a part score the other way.

Transfers opposite 2NT

After a 2NT opening, or a sequence such as 2♣ – 2♦ – 2NT, this is the scheme:

3♣	Baron, or Stayman
3♦	transfer to hearts
3♡	transfer to spades
3♠	minor two-suiter

Assessment.   Transfer bids gain in two important ways. First, the no-trump opener plays many more hands, protecting his tenaces from the opening lead; second, many more sequences become available to present an accurate picture of the responding hand.

TWO OVER ONE GAME FORCING

Even in the Acol world the standard for a two-level response has risen over the years. Where a shapely 6-count might once have qualified, nowadays something approaching a 10-count is expected. In the US there is a large body of opinion carrying this one stage further, making a two-level response game-forcing. Such a method is possible only when you play a *Forcing 1NT Response*, with which you can cover all the lesser responding hands.

Assessment.   You gain more space for game and slam sequences at the expense of less accuracy when responder holds a hand in the 10–12 region. The method must still be rated as 'experimental'.

UNPENALTY DOUBLES

This is a device to help the defending side judge whether or not to sacrifice against a slam. Suppose that your side has been bidding diamonds at a high level and the opponents reach 6♡. Using unpenalty doubles, the next player will pass if he thinks he has 0 or 2 defensive tricks, double with one. After a pass, his partner will defend 6♡ if he has 0 or 2 defensive tricks himself, sacrifice with 1 trick. After a double by the first defender, his partner will leave in the double only if he has a second defensive trick himself.

Assessment.   The scheme looks neat but the snag is that one never knows quite what will be a defensive trick. Just a queen opposite a jack perhaps . . .

UNUSUAL NO-TRUMP

Since a player with a strong hand has the option of doubling an opening bid, a 2NT overcall (or 1NT by a passed hand) indicates a two-suiter in the two lowest unbid suits. This sequence is common:

South	West	North	East
1♡	2NT		

West shows a minor two-suiter. Some players make the call on quite unsuitable hands, with suits such as Kxxxx and Qxxxx. This is a silly idea; apart from risking a large penalty, such a call will give information to the eventual declarer when (as is likely) the opponents win the auction.

The no-trump call is unusual in this auction too:

South	West	North	East
Pass	1◇	Pass	1♠
1NT			

Since South passed originally he must now be showing a distributional type, at least 5–5 in clubs and hearts. Some partnerships would treat 1NT as unusual even if South had not already passed.

South	West	North	East
1♠	2◇	2♠	No
No	2NT		

This is rather a different type. West indicates a second suit in what is probably a 6–4 hand. Since he could have bid 3♣ on the second round to indicate a second suit of clubs, 2NT suggests a 4-card heart suit.

Finally, here is one sequence where 2NT is *not* unusual.

South	West	North	East
1♡	No	No	2NT

East's 2NT is natural, although it may be partly based on a fair minor suit.

Assessment.   There are two ways of playing the Unusual No-trump: as a purely obstructive call which may occasionally lead to a profitable sacrifice, or as a more serious attempt, on quite a strong hand, to compete for the contract. It is foolish to mix the two together, so that partner never knows how high to go. On the whole, we prefer to regard the overcall as a genuine attempt to fight for the contract, except perhaps at favourable vulnerability, where it may be regarded as a risky challenge.

VOID-SHOWING JUMP

Once you have agreed a suit, a jump in a new suit indicates a void there. This is a typical example:

South	North
2♡	3♡
3♠	5♣

North holds:

♠ K872   ♡ K1054   ◇ QJ972   ♣ –

A call of 4♣ would have been a normal cue bid; the jump to 5♣ proclaims a void club.

Sometimes it is the jump itself which sets the trump suit.

South	North
1◇	1♠
4♣	

South shows an excellent spade fit and a void club.

Assessment.   In the first sequence most players would assume that responder was showing a void. In the second sequence 4♣ certainly agrees spades as trumps but could have various secondary meanings. Rather than indicating a void club, it could show a singleton club (Splinter Bid) or could be simply a cue bid. Either of these two meanings is probably more useful than to reserve the call to show a void.

WEAK TWO BIDS

Players who have not adopted the Multi-coloured Two Diamonds may play 2♡ and 2♠ (and possibly 2◇) as weak two bids, usually in the 6–10 point range. These calls work best when the values are mainly in the suit called.

	(1)		(2)		(3)
	♠AQ9842		♠Q97432		♠2
	♡7		♡A103		♡KQ10643
	◇J102		◇95		◇4
	♣J92		♣K4		♣K10876

Hand (1) is an ideal weak 2♠ opener, with 6 of the 8 points in spades. On (2) you might open 2♠ in third or fourth position, but to do so in first or second risks playing in 2♠ one down, with 4♡ easy. The danger with 2♡ on (3) is that your playing strength is too good; give partner the ace of clubs and another ace and you would be close to 4♡. It's better to pass for the moment.

Responding to weak twos. It is usual to play 2NT as a forcing response, nominally agreeing the opener's suit. Over 2NT the opener may express a minimum by rebidding his suit or bid another suit to suggest values there and better than a minimum hand.

A new suit by responder (such as 2♡ – 3♣) is forcing; a raise in the opener's suit (2♡ – 3♡) primarily defensive, but capable of trapping an over-eager opponent. You may try it with K-x of partner's suit and a 12-count.

Assessment. If you study the records of high-level encounters, especially in America, you will come across numerous examples of weak two bids that are not just weak but paralytic. It is *very* doubtful whether such tactics are sound. After all, the Italians won the world championship for almost ten years in succession without ever abandoning the usual standards. Played sensibly, weak two bids are an arm of the attack.

Inevitably you will be tempted to say at times, 'We play this convention differently at my club. We . . .' Yes, we realise that. But obviously it is impossible to cover all styles. This chapter will have done its work if it helps you to judge which conventions are worth considering, which are not. When someone suggests a cute idea, bear in mind always that if you use a bid in a conventional sense its value as a natural call is lost. Weak jump overcalls (page 69) are an example. If you adopt this style, which is admittedly popular in some places, you have to scurry around to find a solution on those hands that are right for an intermediate jump overcall.